# Developed Through Dirt

# DEVELOPED THROUGH DIRT

Charity Morris

*Developed Through Dirt*

Charity A. Morris

Copyright © 2015 by Charity A. Morris

Published by Scribe Publications
404-919-1931
http://www.scribepublicationsinc.com

Cover Art by Michael Kopkas

Cover Design by Bernard Granger

All rights reserved. This book or parts thereof may not be reproduced in any form, stored in a retrieval system, or transmitted in any form by an means - electronic, mechanical, photocopy, recording, or otherwise - without prior written permission of the publisher, except as provided by United States of America copyright law.

Unless otherwise identified, scripture quotations are from the Holy Bible King James Version, Cambridge, 1769. Used by permission. All rights reserved.

Scripture quotations marked AMP are taken from the Amplified Bible, Copyright (c) 1954, 1958, 1962, 1964, 1965, 1987 by The Lockman Foundation. Used by permission. (www.Lockman.org).

Scripture quotations noted NLT are from the Holy Bible, New Living Translation. Copyright (c) 1996 and 2004. Used by permission of

Tyndale House Publishers, Wheaton, Illinois. 60190. All rights reserved.

Scripture quotations noted MSG are from the *The Message*. Copyright © 1993, 1994, 1995, 1996, 2000, 2001, 2002. Used by permission of NavPress Publishing Group.

Scripture quotations noted TLB are from The Living Bible copyright © 1971 by Tyndale House Foundation. Used by permission of Tyndale House Publishers Inc., Carol Stream, Illinois 60188. All rights reserved.

Scripture quotations noted (ESV) are from The ESV® Bible (The Holy Bible, English Standard Version®) copyright © 2001 by Crossway, a publishing ministry of Good News Publishers. ESV® Text Edition: 2011. The ESV® text has been reproduced in cooperation with and by permission of Good News Publishers.

Any name referencing satan will not be given the respect of capitalization, even at the risk of improper sentence structure.

ISBN-13: 978-0996782401

Library of Congress Control Number: 2015951656

Printed in the United States of America.

## Dedication

This book is dedicated to all who are contending with the faith. Be not weary in doing well. In due season, you will reap a bountiful harvest if you don't faint and give up.

## Acknowledgement

Firstly, to My Lord and Savior, Jesus Christ, without whom I am nothing. Thank You for seeing fit that I partake of Your suffering, that I may *know* You! I love You with my life, for the rest of my life!

To my family and friends, thanks for the support and trusting the gifts and talents God has unearthed in me.

Gary, thank you for loving me, encouraging me and pushing me, even though I gave you many side eyes and mumbled under my breath! You are truly God-sent!

To my enemies, I thank you for every challenge. You propelled me into the presence of God and helped me *Develop through Dirt*!

## Table of Contents

Forewords                                                                 9
Introduction                                                             14
Prologue                                                                 21
1  Cultivating the Will to Live                                          26
2  Trusting Him in the Developmental Dark                                30
3  Compost Piles                                                         47
4  Perfected Through Pressure                                            67
5  The Pain of the Process: Hurting But Not Hopeless                     88
6  Buried Alive                                                          98
7  Familial Dirt: The Promise, the Pit, the Prison, the Palace          107
8  Rich Dirt, Bountiful Harvest                                         118
Endnotes                                                                133
Prayer of Salvation                                                     135

# Foreword

My first encounter with Charity Nelson Morris, and the day we met, was the day I heard her speak for the first time. When I asked about the speakers for our women's meeting, she was pointed out to me. I have a vivid memory of seeing her for the first time: Short, cute, round chocolate face with expressive eyes. Nicely appointed in a tailored suit, she chatted with some other young women as they emerged from the women's bathroom at our church. I really don't remember seeing her prior to that time, and wondered who was this 'little young thing" that was going to be addressing the women that morning.

I am 6'2 in bare feet, and what I remember most upon seeing her for the first time, is how this small woman seemed to walk and have a presence of a person my size. There was a confidence that exuded from her that was rare, for someone so young, and yes, so small in stature. However, once she took the dais and began to address the women, it was clear; God had deposited much in her pint-sized package! Charity addressed the women with authenticity and authority, masterfully delivering the Word of God. I am not impressed by much, but she definitely had my attention!

After the meeting, I introduced myself and shared how I had enjoyed her message. She graciously thanked me and a conversation ensued. Somehow the conversation turned to my business' need for organization. Before I knew it she was volunteering her services to assist. Numbers were exchanged, and as the saying goes, 'the rest is history.'

Charity became like a little sister to me. In our times of fellowship, we talked, we prayed. Seldom superficially; always out of concern for the church and the Body of Christ. And I learned in the process that she was by no means ordinary. With a penchant for the Word and the things of God, her heart's desire was always for the furtherance of the Kingdom – to aid others, to see them grow, and to do her part in the furtherance of the gospel. She was a poster child for Matthew 6:33 (Amplified version): "But seek (aim at and strive after) first of all His kingdom and His righteousness (His way of doing and being right), and then all these things taken together will be given you besides. For someone her age, I found her to be refreshingly committed. But this love, this devotion, and apparent anointing upon her life, would cost her, and dearly.

I witnessed my sister face challenge after challenge, attack after attack – personally, professionally, in ministry. Some of the things she faced were unbelievable. The enemy was after her with a vengeance! She was given every reason to give up, turn coward, and run. But she would not!! More often than not, she continued to serve, continued to smile, yet suffered in silence ...but fought like a prize fighter!!!! Petite in stature but powerful in God, Charity knows who she is, she knows her God and has been qualified by Him to share His truths in a way that is impactful. She has proven over and over, as she has "gone through the fire," with perseverance and trust in God, you can win.

The Christian life can be a struggle, and it can be painful. And yes, as a soldier in the trenches of war, you will get dirty! But take heart! There is unseen richness in the soil that God allows us to go through and cover us at times. As you leaf through the pages of this book, you may be down, you may be "under it," you may feel like lying down and giving up. I pray that as you read Charity's trials and triumphs in "Developed Through Dirt," you will see that through faith and patience, the resurrection and rebirth that springs forth from your time in the dirt and mud will bring forth growth that can be glorious!

In awe of Him,

Yvette Wright Gauff

Actress, Singer, Philanthropist

# Foreword Part 2

Charity Nelson Morris is a scholar, anointed vessel used mightily of the Lord, intelligent, beautiful, and above all else, a daughter of the Lord.

In her book, she revisits the place of pain, hurt, and even feelings and emotions of spiritual abandonment. I know Charity personally, and saying she is a strong young lady is an understatement.

The question is, who really knew the depth of the various attacks she dealt with, she struggled through, and with the Lord's help, ultimately triumphed over?

This book is a wake-up call to the Church. Do not allow another smiling face to pass you by without taking time to understand the depth of what is really in a person's heart. May this book stir you and cause you show forth the love and compassion of the Lord. Although attacks are real in the lives of Christians, however the Lord's love and power is greater than anything one may face.

May the anointed pages of this book minister to you as Charity allows herself to be transparent and vulnerable, yet triumphant.


In God's love,


Prophetess Leticia Lewis

Founder, Majestic Ministries International and

International Covenant Christian Chamber of Commerce

# Introduction

The struggle is real.

The pain...REAL!

The torment...REAL!

The tears...REAL!

The sleepless nights...REAL!

BUT what is just as real and even more real is the truth that God loves you and has a plan for the pain that you have suffered and will yet endure. For every situation you face, there is a promise in God's Word that will help you get through it. I will not promise you overnight deliverance or even deliverance in a year. What I can promise, WITHOUT A SHRED OF DOUBT, is that God has already pre-planned your victory and deliverance, but you have to walk out the process. In case you didn't know, God is very willing to interrupt your happiness and comfort to *complete that good work which He has begun in you* (Philippians 1:6)!

Just as manure enriches soil to promote growth, just as sand paper smooths out rough surfaces, just as intense fire refines gold, just as heat strengthens and tempers steel, just as boiling water brings out the flavor of tea, so too must we enter times of adversity, fire, pain and suffering if we are going to be fully refined in our character and drawn to a deeper connection with the Lord Jesus Christ. Believe me when I say there is much brokenness and pain that comes through suffering and adversity, yet the end results far outweigh the pain experienced.

Each of us have our moments of crying, kicking, screaming and thoughts of 'why me' as we go to our crosses. While in the Garden, even the perfect One, Jesus the Christ, Jesús Cristo, Emmanuel, Son of God, cried and didn't want to face the Cross and endure the suffering that He was destined to face. The Word tells us in John 12:24 *unless a kernel of wheat falls to the ground and dies, it remains only a single seed, but if it dies, it produces many seeds.*

The pain of the process will cause you to cry out in agony. The pressure of the process will try to force you to denounce God's purpose and promise. Some days you will feel so alone and abandoned by God and everyone else that you will think nothing and no one is working in your favor. There will be times when it seems like the world is against you. There may be a time on your path to the promise that you will want to completely abandon it all and say God take me now. There will be days when you won't understand. There will be days when you question God and His sovereignty.

Trust me, I do understand where you are and what you are experiencing. I have gone through what seems like every facet of the temptation to throw in the towel. I questioned God, I was angry with God, I even yelled at God because the pain seemed unbearable. There were days when I physically did not have strength to get out of the bed, yet alone do anything else. No matter what I felt or faced, my foundational truth and belief system always took me back to what I knew deep down... that God really is God, His mercies are new every morning and that someway, somehow this will *all come together and work for my good* (Romans 8:28).

During the thick of my challenges, one of my go-to scriptures was and continues to be Hebrews 13:5-6 (Amp):

> *$^{5b}$for He [God] Himself has said, I will not in any way fail you nor give you up nor leave you without support. [I will] not, [I will] not, [I will] not in any degree leave you helpless nor forsake nor let [you] down (relax My hold on you)! [Assuredly not!]. $^6$ So we take comfort and are encouraged and confidently and boldly say, The Lord is my Helper; I will not be seized with alarm [I will not fear or dread or be terrified]. What can man do to me?*

With every obstacle that you and I face and conquer, confidence is being built and faith is being developed in God's trustworthy ability to deliver.

This book was written from a very personal place. I've felt it, feared it, and fought through it. My choice to become vulnerable is to ultimately show you that God has a purpose for every component and aspect of your life, to tell you that God will defy the words impossible, hopeless, useless, garbage, junk, worthless and meaningless. My candor comes from a yearning to see God morph the pain in your life to a perfectly priceless portrait that tells of His goodness, grace, and grandeur.

I'm not here to share all of my business; if I wanted to do that, I could have easily sounded off on social media. Speaking of which, keep your business off social media. Like me, you may be struggling with finding the right words to explain what is happening. Could it be this is not the time for you to talk? Sometimes, you talk too much. Stop living your life and defining your worth based on the volume of posts, the number of likes and the number of comments and shares. You're going through enough. Adding unnecessary warfare by talking too soon or too much will only worsen the situation. At times, God will give you instructions and guide you down a path that does not make sense first to you, yet alone to anyone else around you. Remove the general population out of your business; some will try to talk you out of your blessing and miracle because the steps you take don't align with their finite process in their finite mind. Pray and talk to one or two trusted friends, a counselor, advisor, or mentor. You don't need everyone in your world giving you advice or even worse, taking joy in your temporary pain. (This soap box moment has been brought to you by Nelson Notables™).

With this book, I aim to be transparent and completely real with you. I want you to know it will get dark. It will get lonely. It will get nasty. It will get smelly. At times, you will want to cave in, quit, throw in the towel, cuss, kick the dog, drown the goldfish and knock over the trash can. I felt all those things and more. Get it out...cry if you must, scream if you must, punch a bag, take kickboxing to let it out (just leave the dog out of it). Do whatever it takes to not keep all of those thoughts, feelings and emotions bottled inside of you.

Find some type of safe release. Once you get it out for that moment (oh, it's no guarantee that those thoughts and feelings won't return), keep on fighting, keep moving forward. Don't camp out at the place of pain. Don't build an altar for hurt. Don't make a home for grief. Don't pitch a tent and build a fire for depression. These are not your friends. They are not there to add to the quality of your life so stop making it comfortable for them to stay in your life. The moment you open the door, they will quickly invite their compadres…fear, doubt, defeat, sickness, hatred, rage, death and any other partner that will add to your misery. Resist the temptation to let them in your space. FIGHT BACK! When that negative, evil thought comes, FIGHT BACK with the Word.

> *Revelations 12:11 – "And they overcame him by the blood of the Lamb, and by the word of their testimony."*

In this book, I will use my personal experiences, the Word of God and several common processes, such as science, nature, and cooking to help illustrate spiritual processes. Understanding many earthly processes and strategies helps me to get an idea of what is happening in the Spirit. It by no means provides a full understanding, but the concept gives me a glimpse of what I am facing on a larger scale.

For instance, look at the pruning process. Pruning is vital to a plant's health and growth. An astute gardener prunes the branches of their plants to help correct irregular growth habits and even causes the flowers and fruit size to increase exponentially; it also assists in preventing disease and insect infestation.

Pruning is especially important if you plan to transplant a plant. Transplants are often messy, uncomfortable and involve cutting the roots. It is only because the plant is experiencing sizeable growth that it's necessary to transplant it into a larger space. For a while, the plant goes through a period of shock because it is being moved (better put, disturbed from what was familiar to it, the place where it was settled and comfortable) to a new environment where the roots have to resettle.

The cutting away during the pruning and transplanting process is by no means random. The gardener strategically watches the leaves and branches that are draining the life source from the plant and removes the dead weight. If left untouched, the diseased portion can spread to other parts of the plant, retard growth and could even bring death to the entire plant. The same concept is true spiritually.

> ***John 15:1-2*** – *[1] I am the true vine, and My Father is the vinedresser. [2] Every branch in Me that does not bear fruit, He takes away; and every branch that bears fruit, He prunes it so that it may bear more fruit.*

What may initially appeared to be opportunities, good relationships, concepts, things and thinking that seemingly shifted or suddenly disappeared altogether from your life is actually God doing His due diligence as the Vinedresser. Cutting those things, places and people from your life is needed to prevent them from draining your life source. It's not that He's trying to hurt you. God is actually positioning you for progression, promotion, and possession.

Pruning is necessary for growth and maturation in God. You may find that your circle of friends becomes smaller, the things you do are changing, the places you go are changing, and even your thought life will change as you spend more time in the Word and seeking the plan of God for your life. It's not that some people or things were bad, but for where you are going, they were not a fit for your future, so the pruning was necessary.

As you read and relive part of my journey, I pray that you will be inspired to walk in faith and stay in faith no matter what comes your way. I pray that my life as well as revelational truths from God's Word and hidden wisdom from life's processes will bless you and help you understand that you are being developed not debilitated. My desire is that your pain will propel you into your passion and that the pressure push you into your purpose, as it did for me.

# Prologue

Nervously, I wait in the hallway of the courthouse. No matter what I eat or drink, I can't shake this cotton-mouth syndrome I have. Sweaty palms and a shaking leg has now been added to this tense mix. Finally after what felt like an eternity, they call my name...."Charity Nelson, please step this way."

I walk into the cold room and felt the piercing, judgmental stare from every glaring eyeball. As I go down the aisle towards the bailiff, I say a quick prayer asking the Lord to help me. Immediately in that instant, other thoughts flood my mind: how did I get here; I'm just a college student who works a lot of hours. My life is school, work and church. My hands are clean; it's not my problem. How did I get wrapped up in this dirty mess of a situation?

I had never been more nervous touching the Bible than at that moment. I take the chair and the questions start. For an hour and a half, I am asked about my role and job function at the place where I am a supervisor. They probed into the records that I and my team members kept, asked about management, the incidents that occurred, the staff and everything else they fancied.

This grand jury is a result of a year-long investigation that had been launched against the company. Because I work so many hours, they concluded that I may have more information than most people so the FBI called me and came to my house to ask questions. For nearly two hours, the agent asked me about the company's operations and people. After he left, I was mentally drained but relieved, thinking it was over; weeks later, he calls and asked me to give a sworn statement in front of a grand jury.

Testifying in front of this federal grand jury almost made me lose bodily functions. Not because I did anything wrong but because I know the implication of what I say could be detrimental to the lives and well-being of so many people. The fear of being black-balled by the company far outweighed the fear of saying no to being questioned by the FBI in my home and then being asked to testify at the deposition.

Upon returning to work, I just knew this was the end of my career with the company. I wait and wait for management to escort me out the building. Nothing happens. Shocked and nervous, I work without any interruptions or questions from people. At the end of the day, I finally breathe a long awaited sigh of relief.

Months are going by without any trepidation. Then my manager asks me to come into his office. I think, "Well there goes that streak of peace." I slowly approach his office and prepare to hear those words… "We no longer need your service." I enter his office, jaded and on the defense. Surprisingly, he offers me a job at our west coast facility as the Lab Manager. Imagine the shock and disbelief… a promotion, a very nice salary with perks, and I would not have to live through another dreaded winter in the Midwest. Had I been wearing pearls, they definitely would have been clutched. I ask him to give me some time to think about it. The sinister side of me thinks this is a trap, they are trying to set me up. After I shut down the pessimism in my head, I begin to think…A FRESH START. I would leave behind the hurt, pain and negativity of a co-worker giving me a black balloon with a white face (which caused racial tension amongst our unit). I would leave behind the investigation. No longer will I have to peer over my shoulder in fear. This can be a clean break. A new beginning.

After praying about it, I tell my manager that I will take the position. They are giving me three weeks to pack up and head west. Piece of cake! I am ready for the change of scenery so that was my motivation to make it happen quickly. I don't know anyone, but that was part of the beauty and appeal of this choice.

I am enjoying my job and life that I have here with little to not toil. New friends, new church home, new everything. I am thriving in my career. They are promoting me to middle management; this comes with a sizeable compensation package and undoubtedly more responsibilities. I am now the Lab and Technical Services Manager. Favor is also opening doors at my new church; in a short space of time, I am teaching various classes and mentoring a group of young ladies. I have a feeling that I am being groomed and fast-tracked for something great and I am receiving confirmation from so many people about the illustrious destiny God has for me. My love for God and passion to help others has finally met, converged and exploded and I am enjoying every moment of it. I am unquestionably busy but there is a special grace on me to do it all with ease. Life as I know it is grand and I am loving every moment of it. This is what I experienced for three years…peace, prosperity, promotion in every area of my life.

As time goes on, I begin to feel an uneasiness when coming to work. I know the new year will bring new challenges but I cannot help but wonder what God has in store for me in 2005. Instinctively, I know my time is coming to an end at work; for now, I will pray and ask God to give me peace, but there is no sign of peace. Hmmm…is it time for me to start looking for another job? It's not that the work is difficult or that the people I work with aren't good. It is just an uneasiness, a tension in the air with which I am not comfortable so I will continue to pray for direction.

Mid-February, the Vice President of Operations comes and gives all middle management a two-week notice of layoff. Finally a peace comes. I knew something was up but I just didn't know exactly what it was.

March 1, although it marks my last day here, it feels like my first day of freedom; no longer am I tied to the reminders of the pain I endured with the company. I am happy and looking forward to what God is about to do for me and with me in this new season of my life.

To say I am enjoying my unemployment is a gross misstatement. I now have time to do what I want to do….finally getting caught up on my rest, finally able to visit my friends more frequently and now I am able to give full attention to my volunteerism in ministry.

Months and months begin to pass and no sign of a job; the joy of not working is totally gone. Fear begins to creep in and tell me I've been left out to dry. After fighting for hours to fall asleep, I suddenly awake to sharp pains in my chest. Cold sweats consume my body.

Laying in a fetal position seems to be the best way relieve some of the pain.

Stress…Fear…Worry…Anxiety…Doubt… they are all ganging up on me and trying to take me out of here. For a moment, I think, 'finally, an end to this turmoil. God is finally answering my prayer to take me home to Glory.' In pain, I close my eyes, brace myself, say my final prayers and welcome the conclusion of my life.

# Cultivating the Will to Live

*2 Timothy 3:12*
*In this life, we will suffer persecution.*

Lord, take me NOW! My level of pain and pissedoffedness (yes that is a made up a word) was through the roof. My struggles had begun to have an effect on me physically...I didn't want to eat or I overate, constant headaches, I was tired most of the time yet I really couldn't sleep. There were days when I woke up literally gasping for air, because even breathing was difficult. It felt like I had a seven ton elephant sitting on my chest. To me, the weight of the world, my world, was on my shoulders.

I eventually realized that I was in the thick of major warfare, mostly due to my destiny, some because of poor decisions I made. My will to live was diminishing. the devil was making compelling arguments for me to give up and at many times, I did want to give up because of the pressure that I was under mentally, emotionally, physically, financially and socially. Have you ever gone swimming and took in too much water? If so, multiply that feeling times 100 and you will begin to understand how I felt like I was drowning under my circumstances.

I found myself thinking and eventually saying "what's the point of living for God? Is it really worth all this trouble? I have

## The Will to Live

nowhere to turn, nowhere to go, nowhere to run and hide." Thoughts of being in Heaven popped up more frequently. I knew there was more to life than what I was experiencing but the energy or resolve to fight for it was quickly fading.

No one told me I would cry myself to sleep at night. No one told me about the isolation. No one told me about the insurmountable pain. No one told me about the betrayal from within my personal walls of trust. You couldn't have convinced me that I would lose my home, car, job, and fight to live all within months of each other.

I tried for a while to maintain the "appearance" of everything being ok. I kept on going to church, kept on teaching, kept on serving as a choir leader, bookstore worker, youth ministry leader, media ministry worker and volunteering as other needs arose. Sure I spoke the Word and confessed that a change was going to happen for me, that God would bring a breakthrough in my life. I coated the pain with prayer yet the problems persisted.

The unemployment was close to running out. For many, many months, I was relentless in my job search. I pulled on every network that I knew but no job would come through for me. Doors either closed in my face or never opened at all. Rejection had become reality. I've never gone through this in my life. I never had a problem getting a job. Whenever I applied for a job, I got it, so this concept and season was foreign to me.

After receiving my last check, the only door that opened for me was a secretarial position. My pride was totally shot. How did I,

## Developed Through Dirt

an educated woman who was a manager of a laboratory, become someone's admin? Just when I thought I was at my lowest, the ground gave way and dropped me deeper. I lost that job within a year and was going through heartache and heartbreak from a failed relationship.

Never in a million years did I imagine this was the path that my life would take. After all, I was saved, really saved, since the age of seven. I loved God with all of me. I spent time in prayer, fasting and reading the Word. I served Him in ministry since the age of 10. I travelled with my mother when she had speaking engagements since the age of 15. I went on mission trips to the forsaken third-world countries. I tithed. I gave. I sowed precious seed YET I had hit rock bottom.

In a matter of months, life as I knew it was gone. Job – gone, savings – gone, car – gone, home – gone, some friends – gone, ministry – gone, some family – gone, peace – gone, happiness – gone. I even lost what I had moved to storage. I felt like I was broken into a million pieces. I was numb. I still had a few friends that were supportive of me, but I was in a place where I did not want to talk to anyone, so I shut nearly everyone out of my life. I would not take or return phone calls from most of my family and friends. It hurt too much to even talk and I felt they wouldn't understand. I did not want to waste what little strength I had in explaining what was happening so I just became quiet. My life had solely consisted of going to church and going back to where I was sleeping (I can't even call it home) to job hunt. I got to a point where I was tempted to take my life but I couldn't afford the funeral! I cried out to God and asked Him to help

## The Will to Live

me and deliver me from this horrible pit. My self-esteem and self-worth was at a negative. I had begun to allow the situation to define who I was.

I was not in my right mind; I entertained thoughts of suicide. I now intimately understood what David meant when he said *tears had become my meat day and night* (Psalm 42:3). I felt like that:

> *Day and night I have only tears for food, while my enemies continually taunt me, saying, "Where is this God of yours?"*

I said to myself, *"Something has got to change NOW. This is not me. I have more living to do. This cannot be the end for me. Yes this is horrible but somehow things can change. I don't know how, but things have got to change for me."*

# Trusting Him in the Developmental Dark

*Job 14:14*
*If a man die, shall he live again.*
*All the days of my appointed time will I wait, till my change come.*

Every promise has a challenge and every winner goes through some form of opposition and uncertainty. Many people believe that when storms come, they must be out of the will of God. They feel they've done something wrong. They've disobeyed and God is not pleased with them. While this may be true, it is not the sole reason for you experiencing tough times. Jesus was under attack from the time He was brought to this earth until His death and He was in the perfect will of God. The Word says, *in the world you have tribulation and trials and distress and frustration; but be of good cheer [take courage; be confident, certain, undaunted], for I have overcome the world. I have deprived it of power to harm you and have conquered it for you* (John 16:33 Amp).

God will give you assignments and destinies that will lead to so many roadblocks, storms and challenges that it will seem impossible for you to complete. That is done by design. He will put something in your spirit that you cannot do on your own. The completion of your assignment will require dependence on Him and trust of His guidance, even when His directions sound strange. At

## Trusting in the Dark

times, God will have you taking steps and move in a way that seems out of step with your present situation yet it is in total alignment with where you will be in your future.

I knew God had a massive plan for my life but I didn't know the path He would lead me on encompassed such pain, heartache and pressure. In my struggle is when I began to truly learn the difference between belief and trust. To say I believed God would be a serious understatement. I believed every aspect of the Bible; I believed everything I've ever read and learned about God. Did I trust Him? With my lips I said yes, but when the pressures came, it showed me that my trust needed to be fortified. I trusted my job, I trusted my education, I trusted my talents and abilities, I trusted my bank accounts, I trusted my investments and retirement plans. When all those things were gone, God was still there asking me to trust Him.

Imagine you are at the top of the Grand Canyon and there is a tight rope stretching across the mammoth wonder of the world, from one side of the Canyon to the other side. A professional rope walker, who is highly skilled at his craft, is about to walk across, as he has successfully done so many times. You have heard about him, read about him and have seen him do this death-defying feat by himself as well as with others. This time you are there to experience it live and in color. He turns to you and asks: "Do you believe I can get across this Canyon without falling?" You answer: "Absolutely! I've seen and read about the many times you've performed this over and over again. I've also seen you take others with you to the other side safely. I don't know how you do it or how it's even possible but you manage to pull it off every time." He then says "ok, join me; come with me to the other side." Therein lies the difference between belief and trust. Belief says I know you can do it. Trust says I am so convinced that I will join you. Trust is putting action to your belief and faith.

I have read in the Word of all the miraculous acts God had performed. I saw Him deliver my mother from cancer. I witnessed Him bring my nephew out of a coma, even after him flat-lining twice. Yet when it came time to put feet to my faith, fear initially seized and immobilized me. While in the heat of the battle, I did not recognize how fear had neutralized my faith. Because my focus was on the wrong thing, my faith had begun to weaken and eventually cause me to be momentarily motionless. The enemy's challenges will always come to defy your faith and make a mockery of what you believe.

When the tests and trials came, instead of staying in faith and rejoicing at the opportunity of making full proof of my faith, I cried and questioned God immediately; I was allowing the enemy to make a fool of my faith. I was looking through the wrong lens. I had allowed the enemy's strategy of shock and awe to weaken my stance. Shock and awe is a military tactic that launches consecutive rapid attacks on its opponent, rendering them nearly powerless and in fear of another attack, to the point of shutting down all or part of the opponent's society and the ability to fight[1]. These back to back attacks are heavily reliant on overwhelming power, keen battlefield familiarity and maneuvers, and enormous displays of force to paralyze the opponent's

## Trusting in the Dark

perception of the battlefield and destroy its will to fight. Rapid dominance, as it is also termed in the military, seizes control of the environment and so overload their enemy's perceptions and understanding of events that the enemy would be incapable of resistance at the tactical and strategic levels[2]. Total rapid dominance disrupts mean of communication (prayer), transportation (direction), food (The Word) and water supply (Holy Spirit).

This is exactly what I was facing…rapid fire attacks from the enemy that shook me to the point of being paralyzed with fear of the next attack. I had placed more focus and emphasis on the pain instead of the promise. When I stopped crying long enough to realize that the attacks were about my destiny, I began to refocus on what God was working in and through me. Each attack was strategically allowed to reveal what was in me and what was needed to mature me.

During my season of brokenness, it felt like I was learning how to walk all over again. I was truly learning how to live what I read. No longer was 2 Corinthians 5:7 another scripture that I read (*for we walk by faith and not by sight*). Now I was putting feet to my faith. One day in particular, God began to share with me the difference between faith and fear. One way that the Holy Spirit explained faith and fear to me was through an acronym. Faith is **F**ollowing **A**ll Instructions **T**hrough **H**ardships. Fear is a **F**ailure to **E**ngage in an **A**ppropriate **R**esponse.

Faith and fear are battling for control. Which one assumes dominance is dependent on the choices you make.

## Developed Through Dirt

- Faith activates, fear debilitates.
- Faith detonates, fear defuses.
- Faith masters, fear enslaves.
- Faith charges forth, fear is stagnant.
- Faith is we're well able, fear is they are bigger than us.
- Faith is "give me this mountain", fear is "it's too late now."
- Faith is now, fear is wait and see.
- Faith is forceful, fear is frightful.
- Faith is confidence in God, fear is confidence in circumstances.
- Faith knows no defeat, fear knows no victory.
- Faith conquers, fear succumbs.
- Faith sees the future, fear sees the present.
- Faith compels God, fear repels God.
- Faith commands change for the better, fear permits things to worsen.
- Faith speaks life, fear speaks death.
- Faith pleases, fear punishes.
- Faith praises, fear pouts.
- Faith worships, fear worries.
- Faith anticipates, fear is anxious.
- Faith brings tranquility, fear brings torment.
- Faith declares, fear denounces.
- Faith agrees with God, fear questions God.
- Faith proclaims truth, fear ponders facts.
- Faith focuses on the Promiser, fear focuses on the problem.
- Faith mobilizes, fear neutralizes.
- Faith is limitless, fear is constrained.

Once I shook off the initial shock, I regained composure and started thinking and seeing with a clear mind. One of my first actions was to repent for allowing fear to seize me. People, first words are critical and shape the experience you have when terror strikes. I allowed my situations to talk to me without shutting it down. It's not that I should have been in denial about the existence of the hurt, pain and suffering; I should have denied the situations power to govern my life, emotions and actions. Instead of responding with the Word, as Jesus did so many times, I cried out in fear. When you begin to look at your circumstances, you are off-focused, become out of balance and that will lead to you being easily knocked down.

I understood what the disciples had done because of fear. When a great storm arose, the disciples cried out *"Master, carest thou not that we perish."* Why are you asleep (not responding) while we are about to drown in our situation? In Mark 4:35, Jesus told them *"let us go over to the other side and other boats went with them."* The disciples did not anticipate the hardship and near death experience of getting to the other side; after all, Jesus was the One who gave them this command. When He gives you a promise or asks you to do something, He will provide protection for that purpose. He was fully aware of the attacks that would come against them YET Jesus had full faith that they would reach the other side.

The greatest danger to these disciples was not the storm; it was their fear and doubt. the devil will use doubt to make us question the integrity of God, discouragement to make us question the goodness of God and distractions to make us question the sufficiency of God.

## Developed Through Dirt

The ship was filling with water and the disciples were filling with fear, worry and doubt. Jesus was right where God wanted Him to be but the disciples had forgotten who they had right beside them. They had more faith in the storm's power to take them out than in Jesus' power to take them over to the other side. First Jesus rebuked the wind. Then He spoke to the sea *"Peace, be still."* The phrase "peace, be still" literally means to be muzzled, completely silenced or kept in check[3]; Jesus completely shut the mouth of the storm and crippled its ability to cause terror.

If you read closely, there were multiple miracles that occurred. There was the miracle of the wind, but there was also the miracle of the waves. Normally, when the wind comes to a rest, the waves typically continue to roll for hours, but in this case, the waves immediately stopped and were still. When Jesus speaks an end to your problem, the power for the storm to harm you is completely neutralized and the after effects to come to a halt.

The latter part of verse 35 says and other boats went with them. There are those who are following you and assigned to you so your choices affect them as well. Please understand, satan is trying to take you out so that those who are waiting for you to come will be adversely affected, discouraged, displaced and ultimately destroyed. What the disciples and I failed to realize was that we were not in the storm because of disobedience but because of obedience to what God had told us to do.

## Trusting in the Dark

While in the storm, both the disciples and I spoke out in fear. As can been seen, it is **_VITALLY_** important to choose your words wisely when under pressure. The Word tells us in James 1:19 to *be quick to hear* (event happens), *slow to speak* (processing it in your mind), and *slow to anger* (reaction/response to the event). Jesus was our perfect example and showed us how to respond.

> *Matthew 4:1-10 – Then Jesus was led by the Spirit into the wilderness to be tempted by the devil. $^2$ After fasting forty days and forty nights, He was hungry. $^3$ the tempter came to Him and said, "If You are the Son of God, tell these stones to become bread." $^4$ Jesus answered, "It is written: 'Man shall not live on bread alone, but on every word that comes from the mouth of God." $^5$ Then the devil took Him to the Holy City and had Him stand on the highest point of the temple. $^6$ "If You are the Son of God," he said, "throw Yourself down. For it is written: "'He will command His angels concerning You, and they will lift You up in their hands, so that You will not strike Your foot against a stone." $^7$ Jesus answered him, "It is also written: 'Do not put the Lord your God to the test." $^8$ Again, the devil took Him to a very high mountain and showed Him all the kingdoms of the world and their splendor. $^9$ "All this I will give You," he said, "if You will bow down and worship me." $^{10}$ Jesus said to*

## Developed Through Dirt

*him, "Away from Me, satan! For it is written: 'Worship the Lord your God, and serve Him only."*

Each time satan came at Jesus with a test, Jesus used the Word to defeat him. Jesus didn't ignore satan or think him away or run from him or try to fight with anything in the natural. He used the Word. Because the Word of God is infallible, it is the greatest weapon to use against the enemy.

It is also interesting to note that in Matthew 4, it was no coincidence that right after Jesus had a glorious moment of the Father bragging on Him at His baptism, He was immediately led into the wilderness for a time of testing. This was not the first time this occurred. It was no happenstance that God doted on Job (Job 1:6-8) and how he was blameless and loved God passionately and soon after began to experience trouble. Could it be that God is bragging on you too as He did with Jesus and Job prior to their tumultuous tests? Think about it. The enemy would love nothing more than to prove God wrong, so he will do whatever it takes to break you. But fear not, Jesus has already guaranteed you the victory. You are not fighting for victory, you are fighting from the place of victory because you are *seated with Him in heavenly places* (Ephesians 2:6). Jesus said in Luke 22:31, *"satan has asked to sift all of you as wheat but I have prayed for you that your faith may not fail."* In one of my favorite chapters in the Bible, John 17, Jesus is praying for His disciples:

*⁹ I pray for them: I pray not for the world, but for them which Thou hast given Me; for they are Thine.*

## Trusting in the Dark

*$^{15}$ I pray not that Thou shouldest take them out of the world, but that Thou shouldest keep them from the evil.*

The prayer was not to keep them from testing and trouble but to keep them ***through*** the testing and troubles.

I began to comprehend that the warfare I was experiencing was much bigger than I realized. It was not about what I was seeing, feeling and touching naturally. This was a fight for my destiny. The enemy wanted to make a mockery of the prophecies I received about the purpose God had for me and about the power and authority that I had begun to operate in through ministry and my career. After gaining the proper perspective, it angered me that I didn't immediately respond in faith as I should have. Oh but don't worry, there were other opportunities that would come to test my faith.

So desperate for a change, I went back to the basics. The only thing I knew to do at that point was pick up my Bible and read. What literally saved my life was the Word. Day and night, night and day, I read the Bible. It had become my food, my lifeline.

I began to build myself back up through the Word. Little by little, moment by moment, God's grace was sustaining me. My spiritual muscles were getting stronger as I spent more time reading and praying. I was starting to gain more strength to stand and believe God's Word again. I began to trust God again to deliver me. The more I read and prayed, the more I was convinced that things will work out for me.

## Developed Through Dirt

The Lord began to remind me of the various prophecies and words I had received. I began to meditate on and rehash them. I started seeing myself as the victor and not the victim. I changed how I viewed people who were a challenge to me. Instead of seeing them as my adversary, I started looking at them as God-sent sand paper that was used to smooth out the rough edges in my life. At times, God will use someone who is an authority in your life to bring difficulty...your manager, your parents, your mentor, your pastor or your spouse. The first reaction by nature is offense and anger. There may not be any rhyme or reason why they are treating you unjustly other than God desiring to draw some things out of you and deposit in you.

I now understand why God hardened Pharaoh's heart when Moses went to him to let his people go. Resistance is used to develop muscles. The same is true in this situation. Just as Judas had a purpose in Jesus' destiny and Pharaoh had a purpose in Moses' life, so too does your pain, adversary and adversities have its proper place. The adversity is used to build character, compassion and Christ-like faith. That was a hard but necessary learning lesson on my journey.

Shots and immunization works in a similar manner. When you receive a shot, it does not feel good and it temporarily inflicts pain; it pierces the skin but what is deposited in you helps to build up a resistance and immunity to foreign forces.

I was also learning how to trust God with my heart. I know He is strong enough to handle the world yet gentle enough to handle my heart, but I didn't readily trust Him with my heart _**completely**_. I was saying I forgive but I was still holding on to the pain, hurt and sorrow. Secretly, a part of me was angry with God for allowing all of this to happen and allowing those who wronged me to get off without any punishment. As my perspective changed, my heart was softened to the point where I was not only able to forgive anyone who had ever wronged me but to pray for them and truly love them inspite of the ill-treatment. Most importantly, I forgave myself. I asked Holy Spirit to help me learn every lesson I'm supposed to learn so that I won't repeat and, even more, so that I may help others. The more time I spent practicing the presence of God, the less I was bothered by my present circumstances.

It would be months before I saw any tangible evidence of the Word working but I had to keep on reading, keep on confessing, keep on believing and keep on trusting. All I knew was I had to try something different. Depression was not my friend. The dark pit was cold, lonely and filled with uncertainty. The more I stopped trying to do it on my own and trusted God's plan, the more I began to experience a peace while in the middle of the storm.

After some time of consistently, relentlessly, and on purpose abiding in His Word and His presence, I noticed changes. First in me, an unexplainable joy and confidence grew. I had no external indication of anything being different YET there was an unshakable inner knowing and joy that change was not only happening but would soon manifest.

**Developed Through Dirt**

Months later, I did get a job as an Administrative Assistant, which I was completely thankful for, AND I was told to find another place to live. Joy and pain was rolled into one heap. Did I cry….well is the Pope Catholic? YES I CRIED but it didn't last as long. It hurt like hell to be put out by a family member but I didn't sink back into a depression. Now I was able to push past that pain and keep progressing forward.

In those dark places, I began to get an intimate, one-on-one schooling of who God is to and for me. Yes I grew up in church, yes I was saved but it's something about knowing Him for yourself and not solely on what others tell you. Paul said it perfectly….. *That I may know Him, in the power of His resurrection, and the fellowship of His sufferings, being made conformable unto His death* (Philippians 3:10). It's not that I **_WANTED_** to get intimately acquainted with the fellowship of His suffering but to walk in the fullness of what He has called me to be and do, I **_MUST_** go through a level of suffering.

Although we will **_NEVER_** suffer and face what Jesus endured, we will follow a similar pattern….there will be a time in your life where you will be betrayed, figuratively beaten, falsely accused, abandoned by family and friends, isolated, embarrassed, publically shamed, mocked by peers, and a time when it looks like all has died. Painful? Absolutely! However, it's all a part of your process.

As tough as it is, you don't want to come out of the process prematurely. The process is designed to stretch and test you so that you will grow and develop into a mature, disciplined person of faith.

## Trusting in the Dark

I know the process can feel daunting and at times you will feel like you are in the belly of a furnace; there will be a season of extreme heat and gross discomfort. You may even seem like you are dying but stay in there. In essence, you are dying. It's a death of what and who you used to be and a transformation to who God has called you to be.

Transformation, in its elemental state, can appear to be unexplainably chaotic until it is well blended with the right components, similar to making a cake. A cake, in its original state of batter, is inedible and looks nothing like the end product, but once it's put in the fire (oven), the process of transformation begins to take place. At times, there's the temptation to open the oven and peek in on the process, but you must trust the timing of the process.

There's a final test to ensure the cake is done….stick a fork/knife in the cake to see if any batter sticks to the utensil. If there is nothing on it, then the cake is ready. We have a tendency to think we are ready for what God has promised us; we think we're done, we're fully developed but the moment you get the "knife test," you're oozing with substance. YOU'RE NOT DONE YET. Until you do not have a reaction and no fear comes out, you need to stay in the fire!

The danger of taking a cake out the oven (fire) too soon is that you run the risk of getting a flat cake that can't be consumed. Sure the outer edge is cooked but the deeper you go, the more you see it's not done thus it's not good for anyone to eat. You then have a choice to either put it back in the oven (if it can be salvaged) or start again.

## Developed Through Dirt

Restarting is a painful reminder that you do not have the full capacity to make all the right choices on your own. Outside of a destiny-driven process, you sometimes suffer and struggle because of the poor choices you made. Some of the pain you may experience is a result of your own selfish, sinful choices; with the choices you make, you have no control over the outcome resulting from your choices. In your haste to make things happen on your own, you end up creating more pain. It's not that God was trying to punish you by keeping something or someone from you, He was merely trying to protect you but your flesh cried out in anguish as if God didn't want you to be happy.

What's worse is that people get upset when they have to reap the consequences of their choices. If you choose to drink excessively over a long period of time, don't be surprised or get angry with God if you get a report of sclerosis of the liver. If you purchase a home that is well beyond your budget, don't be upset if your prayer for supernatural debt cancellation doesn't get answered; don't get angry with God if you are facing a foreclosure. You are overeating, not showing any self-control, but you are shocked when the doctors tell you that you are 50 pounds overweight and now have diabetes and high blood pressure. You know you weren't supposed to get with that man but you go ahead and marry him because you didn't want to be alone anymore and he being rich was an added bonus; why be upset with God when the marriage fails? You didn't know he had HIV and all the money would be spent on medical treatments.

**Trusting in the Dark**

Bad choices come as a result of following the flesh's unrenewed mind. Whichever one (spirit or flesh) you spend the most time gratifying will be the dominant force in your life. If you continue to please the flesh and eat on the things of the flesh, you cannot expect to have total victory in the natural or spirit.

**THE ONE YOU FEED THE MOST WILL LEAD THE MOST.** The more you give it, the more it wants and requires; each time, the demand gets greater and greater. This is damaging because *nothing good comes of the flesh* (Romans 7:18); it will require more, diminishing and depleting your spirit and eventually consuming you.

> *Romans 7:15-18 (NLT) – [15] I don't really understand myself, for I want to do what is right, but I don't do it. Instead, I do what I hate. [16] But if I know that what I am doing is wrong, this shows that I agree that the law is good. [17] So I am not the one doing wrong; it is sin living in me that does it. [18] And I know that nothing good lives in me, that is, in my sinful nature. I want to do what is right, but I can't. [19] I want to do what is good, but I don't. I don't want to do what is wrong, but I do it anyway. [20] But if I do what I don't want to do, I am not really the one doing wrong; it is sin living in me that does it. [21] I have discovered this principle of life—that when I want to do what is right, I inevitably do what is wrong. [22] I love God's law with all my heart. [23] But there is another power*

> *within me that is at war with my mind. This power makes me a slave to the sin that is still within me. ²⁴Oh, what a miserable person I am! Who will free me from this life that is dominated by sin and death? ²⁵Thank God! The answer is in Jesus Christ our Lord. So you see how it is: In my mind I really want to obey God's law, but because of my sinful nature I am a slave to sin.*

So the next time the *bright* idea comes to do things your way and live life according to your fleshly desires (which is anything contrary to the plan and purpose of God), cast it down because in the end it will lead to some form of failure or setback. Remember the enemy does not fight fair. he will lure you to do things that contradicts the plan of God and put in a pretty package that appears to be easier and trouble free, all to pull the bait and switch on you. he will tempt you to make your own decisions and then condemn you for messing up. Don't bite the bait! You have enough battles when you do the right thing. Don't add unnecessary warfare by making choices without the wisdom of the Holy Spirit! Trust God and the path on which He's leading you.

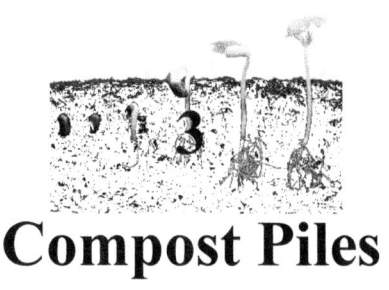

# Compost Piles

*Psalm 118:22*
*The stone the builders rejected has become the cornerstone.*

As a Biology major, I was required to take a Plant Physiology course. In it, I learned quite a bit about the growth and development of plants. In agriculture, skilled farmers and knowledgeable conservationists use compost piles as nutrient-rich fertilizer to aid in the development and growth of seeds that have been planted.

In its simplest form, compost is made of material that most would see as garbage and useless items that have no real value anymore (i.e. leftover foods, manure, paper, leaves, wood chips, grass, kitchen waste, even lent from the dryer and hair clippings from the salon). Manure has been used for centuries as a fertilizer for farming, as it improves the soil structure so that it holds more nutrients and water.

Isn't it ironic how manure, when left in its natural state, is smelly and messy, yet it is used to produce fragrant and beautiful products. The manure (**M**essy **A**ccounts of **N**egative **U**nwanted **R**elentless **E**vents) of your life is prime fertilizer to grow something spectacular. Yes it stinks, yes it's undesirable but it is extremely beneficial. The messy manure in your life is fertilizer to help create an atmosphere of miracles.

## Developed through Dirt

Compost is valuable for the land in several ways: as a soil conditioner because it improves the quality of the soil's composition, as a fertilizer, and as an organic pesticide. Compost improves the structure (integrity) and texture of the soil, enabling it to be easily maneuvered as well as aiding the plant to improve retention of nutrients, moisture, and air.

The compost "trash" is all heaped together in a container and covered to allow decomposition to take place; the wait can range from a few weeks to a few months, depending on the allowance of the process to take place. The decomposition process is aided by shredding the plant matter, adding water and ensuring proper aeration by regularly turning the mixture. Worms and fungi are used to further break up the material.

One will know (discern) the compost is ready for use when the texture has changed to be crumbly, light and fluffy; crumbly soil is made of irregular particles which allows air to penetrate and hold moisture well while allowing excess water to drain away, ultimately allowing for easy cultivation.

The original materials that were used should no longer be recognizable; if much of the original material can still be recognized, then it is not ready to be used. Once it looks like it's ready, it should sit for another three to four weeks to ensure the decomposition process is completed, settled and stabilized. At times, one may be tempted to use the compost before it is ready. However, if incompletely

## Compost Piles

decomposed material is added to the soil, plants will become stunted and it could retard growth.

Well you may be wondering, where is she going with this and what does compost have to do with me. **A LOT**! This natural process of compost creation is similar to what happens in the Spirit. Each of us have faced hardships, failures, hurts, pains of all sorts, shame, embarrassment, rejection and other types of maladies. Do you not know that there is nothing, absolutely nothing wasted in the Kingdom? God will take everything that you've gone through and use it for His glory. Every setback, every failure, every break up, the betrayals, the bankruptcy, the eviction, the divorce, the abortion, the rape, the molestation, the low self-esteem are not wasted experiences. God has a plan to use every experience in your life to testify of His amazing love, grace and power to deliver. I repeat, **THERE IS NOTHING WASTED IN THE KINGDOM**!

While you are going through your varied experiences, God, in His infinite wisdom, is making preparations for use. Little do you realize the pain is being repurposed for something greater. At times, you may feel like you are in a tight, cramped space….and you are. At times, you may feel like things are piling on top of you, one after the other…and they are. At times, you may feel like what was once recognizable and familiar is no longer there…and it's not. At times, you may feel like you are being tossed and turn over and around…and you are.

## Developed through Dirt

As I previously explained the natural process of composting, so it goes in the Spirit. We go through a season of containment, where your situations are piled on top of each other while in a tight place (1 Peter 4:12 NIV – *Dear friends, do not be surprised at the fiery ordeal that has come on you to test you, as though something strange were happening to you*). Then you are forced to sit still for a period of time where nothing is happening; you are in this dark place of silence. Suddenly, you are tossed, flipped and turned to ensure nothing is left in its original state and then it's back to the still, silent phase. Starting to sound familiar? At the right time, you are ready for use, so now you are being spread out (stretched) as top soil and covering to help provide growth and nutrients. God has taken the pain of the past and used it to help others and ultimately grow and advance the Kingdom.

Just as the earthworms were allowed to eat at and break down the material, so too does God allow some things to be consumed. What seemed like it was the devourer sent to consume what you have was actually allowed to assist in your process. In the end, you will have a greater harvest than you could imagine.

So you see, your past is serving as compost to nourish yours and others future. Some people have a big challenge with believing their past can be used to minister to and help people. Many tend to get stuck on the past. What if Paul couldn't get over his past of killing Christians and initially denying Jesus' work on the Cross? What if David couldn't get over his past of being an adulterer, a liar, and a murderer? What if Moses couldn't get over his past of being adopted? What if Joshua couldn't get over the death of his mentor Moses? What

## Compost Piles

if Rahab couldn't get over being a whore? What if Joseph couldn't get over being abandoned by his family? What if Ruth couldn't get past being a widow? What if Jesus couldn't get past not having a biological father? What if Peter couldn't get over denying Christ? Don't allow your past to dictate your future. Don't let a moment in time dominate the permanency of your future.

No matter what your past is, it does not have to define your future. You are not what you suffered. You are good enough. You are the right person for the job. You can complete the assignment God has entrusted to you. Of the billions of people in this world, past, present and future, He willingly chose YOU to fulfill this assignment. Everyone may not understand the vision and where God is taking you but it's not theirs to understand so STOP TRYING TO CONVINCE THEM! Sometimes you just have to shut your mouth and let your works speak for you. Some may judge you according to your past. Follow Jesus' example and keep silent while passing them the stone!

*John 8:7 (NLT)*
*They kept demanding an answer, so He stood up again and said, "All right, but let the one who has never sinned throw the first stone!"*

While you are being developed in your compost process, don't be surprised if you run into unplanned detours and unexpected delays. To be honest, it should be expected. If you are truly allowing God to lead you, it will be down a path that you would not pick!

## Developed Through Dirt

To date, I've not met anyone who takes pleasure in detours or delays. Like so many, one of my greatest pet peeves is traffic and even worse, shifting lanes and detours. Most times, I am on a tight schedule so delays are unwelcomed; I have neither the time nor the patience to wait in traffic. Whether driving or flying, I simply do not like waiting or being delayed. Yes, I am a work in progress!

On one of my flights, which was already delayed, the pilot announced that we had to be diverted and the detour would add an hour to our trip. I became irritable, frustrated and impatient because I had to rearrange my schedule to encompass this delay.

After I got over being irritated, God began to minister to me about delays and deterrents. Sometimes flight gets rerouted to avoid turbulence and bad weather. At times, it is necessary to take a longer path to skip what was heading your way. The detour and delay was really protection and avoidance of potential problems that were ahead of us.

Losing my job and having to live with someone was an unexpected, unwanted yet very much needed detour in my life. I needed to learn true dependence on God and not trust in my career. I needed to learn how to praise through the pressure and worship instead of worrying. I needed to learn true humility so that when God raised me up, I would know it was not because of me but because of His mercy, grace and favor.

## Compost Piles

There was a need that I travel the path of pain so that my will was completely broken and His will and plan was what I desired more than anything and anyone. I needed the detours to help me identify with Christ as Paul so eloquently said, *"that I may know Him in the power of His resurrection and the fellowship of His suffering* (Philippians 3:10) and *"until Christ be formed in me"* (Galatians 4:19).

Life, like air and road traffic, is full of unexpected detours. For a period of time, we experience some level of pleasure and peace and encounter very little trouble, but suddenly we are confronted with a detour. It could be that of job loss, divorce, sickness, abuse, deep disappointment, death or a countless number of other issues.

Very seldom do we know how long the detours will last. In hindsight, it may be more advantageous if we didn't have full knowledge of the challenges that awaited us and their duration. If we know all of the difficulties that lies ahead, every part of the trip would be tainted by the anticipation of trouble.

Our reaction and response to the detour will also factor in the detour's length of time. Complaining, not staying in faith, or attempting to circumvent the process extends our time. We can take the detour and whine about it the entire time. There are far too many people who choose this option. They press on through their troubles, but they are always grumbling. As a result of this complaining attitude, their condition is made worse, their troubles are intensified and the detour is prolonged. This is like the children of Israel who never reached their destination and never received the promise because of their complaining and unbelief.

Most detours are bumpy, turbulent, and contain unpredictable patterns. They always take you out of your way, delay your arrival at your destination, and thus needs to be traversed cautiously and vigilantly; not doing so has the potential to cause major damage. Detours command immense amounts of prayer, patience and perseverance.

*James 5:10 – 11*

*[10] Brothers and sisters, as an example of patience in the face of suffering, take the prophets who spoke in the name of the Lord. [11] As you know, we count as blessed those who have persevered. You have heard of Job's perseverance and have seen what the Lord finally brought about. The Lord is full of compassion and mercy.*

On a detour, it is imperative that you proceed by faith. The road may be one that you have not travelled, therefore you must follow the signs, which promise to get you back on the regular route. David tells us in Psalm 32:8, *"I will instruct you and teach you in the way you should go; I will guide you with My loving eye on you."* Proverbs 3:5 promises us that if we *"trust in the Lord with all of our hearts and lean not to our own understanding. In all of our ways if we acknowledge Him, He will direct our path."* We have this promise

## Compost Piles

from God that in the time of trouble, He is going to work out everything for our good; not for our pleasure or prosperity or popularity, but for our good.

A detour causes you to be thankful for the smooth roads. Do you remember the relief when you got through the last few yards of a tough detour road? In our lives, detours and dark days give way to an appreciation of a life without rough and turbulent travelling. If every day was filled with no adversity and all smiles and sunshine, we would soon lose our appreciation of it. Trouble, sorrow, or afflictions are never enjoyed, but they do help us to take full advantage of the good days.

Learn to accept the detours of life in good cheer, knowing that it won't always be like this. Psalm 30:5 tells us *"Weeping may endure for a night but joy comes in the morning."* During a detour, you may find yourself in a night season and feel completely left alone. Your family and friends seem to be distant even if they are nearby. They may not understand your needs, desires and God-ordained destiny. If you look at major outpourings and the rising of God's chosen vessels, they went through a night season, a time of isolation. There, God was preparing them for the vast future that was set before them. So do not despise the night season. The night season, though dark and filled with uncertainty, is actually a time to rejoice. Whether you recognize it or not, midnight is when the change of day happens. A new day started but because you are in the dark, it is not readily recognized. There are no outward signs that a change has taken place. By the time your eyes recognize and acknowledge the change of day, many hours had already lapsed. Just because you don't see the changes does not mean change has not taken place. It's only a matter of time when all will see a new day has dawned.

One detour that we will all face is that of disappointment. No one in life is free from this detour. We are disappointed in others at some point in our lives. We are disappointed in the failure of our plans. We are disappointed in ourselves. There must be a constant battle against this foe, or we will find ourselves growing bitter, resentful and cynical. In the face of disappointment, we must find a way to keep smiling and trust God. My life is not all I would have it to be. I am at times disappointed regarding circumstances and people, but in it all, I am keenly aware of God's love and grace. Even disappointment has a redeeming feature, for when I am disappointed in myself and in others, I recognize the beauty of mercy.

Mary and Martha in John 11 had a huge opportunity to drown their sorrows in their disappointments. First their brother dies and then Jesus took His slow, sweet time in getting to them. They could have become bitter, angry and resentful towards Jesus. Little did they know God had a larger plan in mind that overrode their desires. He was working a master plan. Although they were *inconvenienced* by this untimely detour, Jesus remained resolute with His plan and instructions. Jesus was a Man in authority yet under the authority of God the Father because He took His instructions from the Father. As a child, our parents would give us instructions that we may not always

## Compost Piles

agree with or didn't always make sense. With limited knowledge and understanding, we would try to get them to explain to us why we had to do certain things or why we couldn't hang around certain people. At that phase in life, we would not fully understand or believe if they told us, plus as a parent, an explanation is not always warranted. "Just do as I tell you to do," is what a child often hears.

If you were like me as a child, you felt the need to know everything and thus a fruitless discussion in trying to understand, followed by slick plotting of trying to negotiate information from my parents ensued. Needless to say, it either got me nowhere or in deeper trouble for talking too much and not obeying them. My finite mind did not see that they were trying to protect me.

The same is true spiritually. There are times when God will give us instructions, have us take a path that seems contrary to what is normal and natural. For most of us, our natural inclination is to question whether we heard God correctly or question why He wants us to take that particular step. Like our earthly parents, He may not give an explanation; He just wants us to do what He asked. One day in my quest to know why, the Father rebuked me and told me my understanding can wait but my obedience cannot.

While on your detours of life, there is going to be a need to obey His instructions and use your spiritual weapons to fight because the enemy will undoubtedly gnaw at your thoughts to try and make you feel like you did not hear God and now you are going the wrong way. God has given you an arsenal of tools to provide protection.

Whether you want to or not, you are involved in the fight of faith. You may as well use your weapons.

### *Isaiah 59:17*

> *He put on righteousness as armor and the helmet of salvation on his head. He clothed himself with robes of vengeance and of godly fury.*

Although we may experience physical elements of the challenges, the fight we face emanates from the spirit realm. Ephesians 6:12 reminds us *"we wrestle not against flesh and blood, but against principalities, against powers, against the rulers of the darkness of this world, against spiritual wickedness in high places. For the weapons of our warfare are not carnal but mighty through God..."* God's weaponry is far more superior to the faulty, earthly weapons used to protect us.

### *Ephesians 6:13-18 (TLB)*

> *[13] So use every piece of God's armor to resist the enemy whenever he attacks, and when it is all over, you will still be standing up. [14] But to do this, you will need the strong belt of truth and the breastplate of God's approval. [15] Wear shoes that are able to speed you on as you preach the Good News of peace with God. [16] In every battle you will need faith as your shield to stop the fiery arrows aimed at you by satan. [17] And you will need*

## Compost Piles

*the helmet of salvation and the sword of the Spirit—which is the Word of God.*

The soldier and weapons that Apostle Paul described in this passage is likened to a Roman soldier. During that era, the Roman soldier was the epitome of a model warrior. They were dressed and ready to fight at any given moment, as we should be spiritually.

*Belt of Truth*

In Bible times, the girdle around the waist held the soldier's garments together; if the belt isn't there, a soldier's movements while marching or engaging in combat could have been hampered. The spiritual significance is that God does not simply want us to point at the truth; He wants us to wear it and have it wrapped about us. Not only does the belt hold everything in place, but it also serves to carry the sheath that holds the sword of the Spirit for easy access.

Truth is vitally important because it will help to ward off the lies and fact-based reports. Just because something seems real, you react to it like it is real, and your emotions act like its real, does not make it real or true. It is fear trying to project onto you what it wants you to believe is truth. As previously mentioned, fear is a **F**ailure to **E**ngage in the **A**ppropriate **R**esponse. Situations are sure to come to challenge your faith. How you respond will let you know if you are in faith or fear. Your response will reveal what is in your heart. When sickness comes, the *appropriate* response is confess the truth that God has already declared...you are healed according to Isaiah 53:4-5.

## Developed Through Dirt

When thoughts of loneliness and depression comes your way, the *appropriate* response is the truth that God will never leave you nor forsake you (Hebrews 13:5). When temptation comes to get you to not give your tithes since money is tight, the *appropriate* response is the truth that God will open up the windows of Heaven as well as rebuke the devourer for your sake (Malachi 3:10-12 NLT).

> *[10] Bring all the tithes into the storehouse so there will be enough food in my Temple. If you do," says the LORD of Heaven's Armies, "I will open the windows of Heaven for you. I will pour out a blessing so great you won't have enough room to take it in! Try it! Put me to the test! [11] Your crops will be abundant, for I will guard them from insects and disease. Your grapes will not fall from the vine before they are ripe," says the LORD of Heaven's Armies. [12] "Then all nations will call you blessed, for your land will be such a delight," says the LORD of Heaven's Armies.*

Speaking the truth is not being in denial of what you are facing but denying the situation the power to dictate your response and control your life.

What will dispel fear? The same thing that would dispel darkness, light (1 John 1:5 – *This is the message I have heard from Him and announce to you, that God is Light, and in Him there is no darkness at all*). I know some of you may say, but I thought perfect

## Compost Piles

love casts out fear (1 John 4:18). This too is correct. God is love **_AND_** God is light. When you get a true revelation of the love of God, His truth will be illumined to you in a greater way.

*1 John 4:16 (ESV)*

*So we have come to know and to believe the love that God has for us. God is love, and whoever abides in love abides in God, and God abides in him.*

*John 3:21*

*But whoever lives by the truth comes into the light.*

I present to you that if you are walking in fear, this is an area where you have not given Jesus total access in your life. Because He is love and light, He will dispel the darkness and bring truth. When you understand, believe and trust the truth of Hebrews 13:5, there is NOTHING satan can throw your way to make you doubt the truth of God's love and ability to deliver you.

*$^{5b}$ for He [God] Himself has said, I will not in any way fail you nor give you up nor leave you without support. [I will] not, [I will] not, [I will] not in any degree leave you helpless nor forsake nor let [you] down (relax My hold on you)! [Assuredly not!]. $^6$ So we take comfort and are encouraged and confidently and boldly say, The Lord is my Helper; I will not be seized with alarm*

# Developed Through Dirt

*[I will not fear or dread or be terrified]. What can man do to me?*

*Breastplate of Righteousness*

The breastplate was an important article of defense that protected the front torso and all of the vital organs from a mortal wound. Wearing the breastplate of righteousness is always in partnership with the robe of Jesus' righteousness. *"I put on righteousness, and it clothed me"* (Job 29:14). The only way we can experience victory against the enemy is through confidence that the righteousness of Jesus covers our hearts and that we are forgiven.

As a child, I was surprised to learn that the breastplate offered no protection to the back. It was assumed that soldiers would not turn their backs toward the enemy to retreat. Likewise, Christians should stand firm and never surrender any ground to the devil. Instead, let the devil flee from your steadfast resolve. *"Submit yourselves therefore to God. Resist the devil, and he will flee"* (James 4:7).

*Feet Shod with the Gospel of Peace*

During those times, the lay of the land was covered with stones, rocks, twigs, thistles and other things that could damage the feet; the opponents would plant in the ground sticks sharpened to a razor point, hoping to pierce the feet of the advancing soldiers. To protect themselves, the Roman soldiers would wear a boot that had a heavy sole so that it couldn't be pierced, because if their feet were

## Compost Piles

pierced, they could not walk (*2 Corinthians 5:7 – For we walk by faith and not by sight*).

We have special shoes for all types of activities and situations. You wouldn't go to play football in basketball shoes. You wouldn't play tennis in baseball cleats. Each of these sports have a specific shoe that has a specially designed function. If it's important in leisure activity, wouldn't it be as, if not more, important during times of war. There are shoes specifically designed for battle. You wouldn't go to war with a pair of alligator shoes. No, you'd be slipping and sliding all over the place! The solider had to have the kind of shoe that would last for long marches, because they would cover tremendous amounts of terrain.

By shodding our feet with the "preparation of the gospel of peace," we declare that the Prince of Peace, Jesus Christ, is triumphant over the powers of darkness. Romans 16:20 says, *"And the God of peace shall bruise satan under your feet shortly. The grace of our Lord Jesus Christ be with you."*

We need to be *at peace* with God. This is the firm foundation beneath our feet. As the saying goes, "No Jesus, no peace. Know Jesus, know peace."

It is also imperative to stand fast *in the peace* of God. This includes casting very care, worry, fear and anxiety on Jesus (1 Peter 5:7) and yielding to His perfect will (Matthew 11:28-30).

# Developed Through Dirt

*Shield of Faith*

The shield was a critical piece of armor because it was used as primary tool for defense. It was typically designed to protect the entire body. In the same manner, faith in the completed work of Christ is our first defense against the enemy of all righteousness. The shield was not held loosely in the soldier's hand, but was firmly strapped to his forearm so he could resist the mighty blows of an enemy's sword without fear of dropping it. Likewise, Christians cannot afford to have a flimsy, fluctuating faith while in the heat of spiritual battle. With the enemy's constant barrage of fiery attacks, the shield of faith repels the firestorm to stop them from making direct contact. Using the shield will help prevent fatal wounds from the battle.

Sadly, many don't use it immediately and end up being wounded on the battlefield because they wait before they decide to use the shield of faith. The moment you see a fiery dart heading you way, put that shield to good use and do everything that is within your power (speak the Word, walk in love, forgive, pray, etc.) to keep as much distance as possible between you and the firestorm of arrows. If you surrender without using your shield, you are, in reality, inviting troubles into your space.

*Helmet of Salvation*

The helmet was the last piece of armor to go on the soldier. It was the final act of readiness in preparation for combat. A helmet was vital for survival, protecting the brain, the command station for the rest

## Compost Piles

of the body. If the head was badly damaged, the rest of the armor would be of little use. In the Spirit, the helmet of salvation is designed to protect your mind, the biggest battlefield in a war! Your mind should not be open to anything and everything.

Because the helmet is related to salvation indicates that satan's blows are directed at the Believer's security and assurance in Christ. This goes beyond receiving Jesus as your Lord and Savior. The scripture text in verse 17 is addressed to Believers so you must already be saved to have it readily available for use. Salvation in this scripture is derived from the Greek word soteria, which means welfare, deliverance, prosperity, preservation and safety[1]. This salvation refers to an ongoing protection from the enemy's attacks of thoughts concerning the welfare of your life; he will try to plant thoughts of "you will never come out of this financial rut," "no one loves you," "you're always being overlooked," "life will get no better than this," "you'd be better off dead than to keep suffering in silence," "no one understands your struggle," "all these church folks talking and singing about how good God is but how is this good God letting this happen to you?" Three of the biggest attacks against the mind are doubt, depression and discouragement, so by donning the helmet of salvation, you are coming against the attacks and negative thoughts that war at your mind.

*Sword of God's Word*

The sword was the most common offensive weapon in a soldier's arsenal. Given it has been mentioned throughout the Bible over 400 times, it shows its importance in winning the fight. This is the very weapon Jesus used to defeat satan during His time of temptation in the wilderness. The Word is the greatest weapon to fight the enemy.

Soldiers had multiple uses for their sword. Their swords were also used for cooking, splitting kindling, and for cutting the ropes that bound their captives to set them free. Likewise, the Word of God is a practical tool for every area of life, as well as in fighting the devil. The Word will bring healing to your body (Isaiah 53:4-5), peace to your mind (Philippians 4:7), increase to your finances (Psalm 115:14), protection for you and your family (Psalm 91), long life (Psalm 91:16) and so much more.

An unused sword, like any knife, became rusty, dull, and pitted. Swords were kept sharp by frequent use, by honing them against a stone (the Rock of Ages), or by rubbing it against another soldier's sword (Proverbs 27:17 – *Iron sharpens iron*). When we get together with other Believers in fellowship and prayer, our swords are being sharpened, causing us to be more efficient and skillful with the sword, which is the Word of God.

# Perfected Through Pressure

*2 Corinthians 4:8*
*We are troubled on every side, yet not distressed;*
*we are perplexed but not in despair.*

We often shout about the promise and end results but complain and despise the process. Our natural tendency is geared to detest pressure. We try to avoid it at all costs, which is a reason why many of us, myself included, are put off by high-pressured sales people. However, there is a need for us to shift our outlook on pressure. When used correctly, pressure can be a positive force: a diamond is created by pressurizing coal, air pressure helps to inflate tires, water pressure helps clean dishes in a dishwasher, and pressure helps launch a rocket off the launching pad. Without the pressure and trials, people tend to become extremely selfish, spoiled and self-sufficient and unfit for the Master's use.

Look at a pressure cooker and how its immense weight is of great benefit. What separates a pressure cooker from an ordinary pot is the controlled environment, the high temperature and the weight of pressure. In a pressure cooker, the air tight environment causes the pressure to increase drastically and raises the boiling point of water. The trapped steam causes the internal temperature to rise from 38 to 250°F using a mere 15 additional pounds of pressure. Because a

## Developed Through Dirt

pressure cooker environment is closed and tightly sealed, vitamins and minerals are not lost, since they are not exposed to the external oxygen (outside influences). The cooking time for most food is about 1/3 the times for those foods cooked in the traditional way and is faster than a microwave.

Some of you can identify with the pressure cooker; the intensity and weight of pressure almost makes your situation seem impossible to escape. But be of good cheer, you won't be in there forever and just as vital nutrients are not lost while in the pressure cooker, so too is God preserving you while under pressure. There is also a relief valve on a pressure cooker to release some pressure when it becomes excessive. The Father is the same way. The Word says God will provide *a way of escape for you* (1 Corinthians 10:13).

Without pressure and opposition, we would not have readily seen the major changes from the Civil Rights movement. Without pressure and opposition, Joseph would not have risen to power and saved his family and the nation of Egypt from the famine. Without pressure and opposition, Jesus would not have been propelled into the greatest part of His destiny. Without pressure and opposition, Paul would not have had some of the greatest revelations and writings of the New Testament.

Pressure, along with trials, tests, and suffering, is a tool God uses to enhance growth and get you into your destiny. Moses was instructed by God to go to Pharaoh (Exodus 5 – 10); he was rejected ten times but each time, his faith and endurance was being developed.

## Perfected Through Pressure

Once they were finally free, Moses and the children of Israel still faced yet another pressurized situation…the Red Sea. His previous victories strengthened him for that current challenge of the Red Sea and if God delivered them before, He could do it again

Apostle Paul experienced a great amount of pain and pressure. Second Corinthians 11 (Amp) gives us a glimpse into what he endured for the sake of destiny.

> *[23] I exceed them [my fellow laborers]; with far more labors, with far more imprisonments, beaten times without number, and often in danger of death. [24] Five times I received from the Jews thirty-nine lashes. [25] Three times I was beaten with rods, once I was stoned. Three times I was shipwrecked, a night and a day I have spent adrift on the sea; [26] many times on journeys, [exposed to] danger from rivers, danger from bandits, danger from my own countrymen, danger from the Gentiles, danger in the city, danger in the wilderness, danger on the sea, danger among those posing as believers; [27] in labor and hardship, often unable to sleep, in hunger and thirst, often [driven to] fasting [for lack of food], in cold and exposure [without adequate clothing]. [28] Besides those external things, there is the daily [inescapable] pressure of my concern for all the churches.*

## Developed Through Dirt

Pressure can be turned into a positive force in your life if you will respond in the right way. Although the pressure from the various trials and troubles brings inconveniences, disappointments, problems, injustices, catastrophes and crisis, pressure is also an indicator that change is happening. It's a sign that a shift of season is on the horizon.

Pressure also reveals our need to depend upon God; if we try to handle it on our own and self-contain the pressure, more stress is created and in some cases, an explosion happens. Your level of thinking and knowing is limited; you may not know where the relief valve is to release the pressure. Your wisdom is limited on the mechanics of handling pressure and stress; you can only go by what you've experienced or seen with others. We become acutely aware of our ineptitude to keep control of the situations. The harder we try on our own, the more chaotic it becomes. Pressure will either have you cry out and pout or cry out in prayer. It is tailored to get rid of the worst in you and make you even better than who you were prior to the pressure.

When the pressure, problems and pain of job loss, illness and relational issues hit me at one time, I eventually retreated to the presence of God and prayed for help and relief. Many times I prayed those David prayers (Psalm 5:1-3, Psalm 25:1-3, Psalm 61, Psalm 37, Psalm 121:1-2). I didn't have the answer; I didn't know how to handle it all or know which way to turn. The only turn I knew was to turn to God for help. No matter how much I prayed, the pressure was not removed and I was not removed from the fiery furnace of affliction.

## Perfected Through Pressure

My reaction to the pressure let me know there was more work to be done; I needed to spend significantly more time in prayer, fasting and reading the Word. The Holy Spirit ministered to me concerning my intake (what I was feeding my spirit and flesh). My initial reaction to the pressure was not Christ-centered. I responded as a mere man instead of someone who knows the Word and knows the outcome is already victory. I allowed my flesh to dominate, which was evident in the words I first spoke.

### *Romans 8:5 (TLB)*

*⁵ Those who let themselves be controlled by their lower natures (the flesh) live only to please themselves, but those who follow after the Holy Spirit find themselves doing those things that please God.*

Walking after the flesh indicates you are living and reacting like a non-believer; the primary response will be one of self-protection and self-preservation. The main motivation is gratifying your desires. People, walking after the flesh is satan's bait. It's as if someone puts a $100 bill on a string and have you reach for it, but the person is steadily pulling the money in his direction; you follow the money and all the while the person is laughing and controlling your actions. And so it goes with satan and fleshly reactions; he's luring and enticing you to follow after the flesh, meaning he's leading, guiding, and controlling the actions in your life. This takes the place of allowing the Holy Spirit to lead and guide your steps.

## Developed Through Dirt

    Continually walking after the flesh is saying with your actions that satan is lord of your life in that situation; he's the dominating influence. You get your instructions from him and you heed to them. Jesus may be your Savior but satan's your ruler; if you don't think so, check the way you are living, talking and thinking. How do you consistently react to negative situations: become spiteful, plot revenge, cuss people out, etc.? How do you respond to someone hurting you? How do you respond to mistreatment? Do you get even? How's your love walk? Do you trust, really trust God? Do you have a consistent devoted daily time of prayer and meditation in the Word? Do you intimately know the Father? Do you give into temptations often? Do you find yourself repenting often and going in circles with the same challenges of life? How much time do you spend entertaining yourself with television, radio, movies, music, friends, going out, etc.? These are just a few questions to get you to begin evaluating your life and see who and what is governing it. I'm not saying all these things are bad but they do have its proper place and everyone is susceptible to regular reactions. The question is do you continue to give in to them?

    I've heard so many people say they can't help themselves, it's an automatic reaction. NO it's learned from previous behavior. It started with an event, you processed the event in your mind, and then you chose which reaction you would take, whether good or bad. You continued to repeat this behavior and pattern in different situations to where it is now becomes a part of you and instantly comes out without you even thinking about it. This is a result of you continually feeding that behavior pattern.

## Perfected Through Pressure

I know that was a bold and brazen thing to say but there comes a time to take ownership of you behavior and start making changes to negative behavior. Easier said than done, I know, yet the good news is that you don't have to do it on your own. God has provided grace and mercy through salvation to help you.

Some people believe that once they give their lives to Christ and become a Christian, they automatically become this holy person, their problems will go away and they won't experience the pressure. Quite the opposite my friend! Because you have declared Jesus to be your Master, Lord and Savior, the attacks are guaranteed to come, the pressure is inevitable and the furnace is unavoidable. However, God will be right there with you through the fire, while in the pressure cooker and through the storms. Honestly, there are some things which are only learned while under pressure.

When the three Hebrew boys were thrown into their pressurized situation, the fiery furnace (Daniel 3:8-30), which was seven times hotter than normal (talk about pressure!), the Son of God showed up in the midst of the situation. He never removed them from the fire but when He did show up, the ropes that bound them were destroyed so that in the midst of the fire, they were freed to praise the Lord. One of the definitions of the anointing is the burden removing, yoke destroying power of God and that is what happened when the Anointed One showed up in the midst of them…the burdensome fire lost its power to kill them and the yokes that bound them were destroyed.

*²⁰ He commanded certain strong men in his army to tie up Shadrach, Meshach, and Abed-nego and to throw them into the furnace of blazing fire. ²¹ Then these [three] men were tied up in their trousers, their coats, their turbans, and their other clothes, and were thrown into the midst of the furnace of blazing fire. ²⁴ Then Nebuchadnezzar the king [looked and] was astounded, and he jumped up and said to his counselors, "Did we not throw three men who were tied up into the midst of the fire?" They replied to the king, "Certainly, O king." ²⁵ He answered, "Look! I see four men untied, walking around in the midst of the fire, and they are not hurt! And the appearance of the fourth is like the Son of God!"*

When they **walked** out of the furnace, not one hair was burned and not even the smell of smoke was on their clothes; nothing and no one was destroyed. When the king saw this, he acknowledged the Great God Jehovah and then promoted them.

*²⁸ Nebuchadnezzar answered and said, "Blessed be the God of Shadrach, Meshach, and Abednego, who has sent His Angel and delivered His servants, who trusted in Him, and set aside the king's command, and yielded up their bodies rather than serve and worship any god except their own God. ²⁹ Therefore I make a decree: Any people, nation, or language*

## Perfected Through Pressure

> *that speaks anything against the God of Shadrach, Meshach, and Abednego shall be torn limb from limb, and their houses laid in ruins, for there is no other god who is able to rescue in this way." ³⁰ Then the king promoted Shadrach, Meshach, and Abednego in the province of Babylon.*

Breakthrough, blessings and promotion are on the other side of the pressure and test! To get to the breakthrough, you have but one job…trust God even if you can't trace Him. The Bible never spoke of the Hebrew boys seeing the Angel of the Lord in the fire with them yet they praised and worshipped God without any evidence of seeing Him or any knowledge of when they would be released from the fire! Even beyond the awesome miracle of the Hebrew boys coming out the fire unharmed, the greater miracle was the king proclaiming God is the Lord over all. Once again, God used the pressure and fire that they endured to bring others to know who He is. It's about you but it's not all about you! God had a bigger plan in mind….to reach others through your pain.

The three Hebrew boys had every opportunity to give in to the king's pressure, but they made up in their minds that they will push (**P**raise **U**ntil a **S**hift **H**appens) and press (**P**ushing through **R**esistance **E**xcuses **S**etbacks and **S**tumbling blocks) their way through the pressure. When you decide to praise God while under pressure and worship God instead of worrying, you give Him an open invitation to step into your situation.

# Developed Through Dirt

## *Psalm 18:3, 9-24*

*³ I will call upon the LORD, who is worthy to be praised: so shall I be saved from mine enemies.*

*⁹ He bowed the heavens also, and came down: and darkness was under His feet.*

*¹⁰ And He rode upon a cherub, and did fly: yea, He did fly upon the wings of the wind.*

*¹¹ He made darkness His secret place; His pavilion round about Him were dark waters and thick clouds of the skies.*

*¹² At the brightness that was before him His thick clouds passed, hail stones and coals of fire.*

*¹³ The LORD also thundered in the heavens, and the Highest gave His voice; hail stones and coals of fire.*

*¹⁴ Yea, He sent out his arrows, and scattered them; and He shot out lightnings, and discomfited them.*

*¹⁵ Then the channels of waters were seen, and the foundations of the world were discovered at Thy rebuke, O LORD, at the blast of the breath of Thy nostrils.*

*¹⁶ He sent from above, He took me, He drew me out of many waters.*

## Perfected Through Pressure

*<sup>17</sup> He delivered me from my strong enemy, and from them which hated me: for they were too strong for me.*

*<sup>18</sup> They prevented me in the day of my calamity: but the LORD was my stay.*

*<sup>19</sup> He brought me forth also into a large place; He delivered me, because He delighted in me.*

*<sup>20</sup> The LORD rewarded me according to my righteousness; according to the cleanness of my hands hath he recompensed me.*

*<sup>21</sup> For I have kept the ways of the LORD, and have not wickedly departed from my God.*

*<sup>22</sup> For all His judgments were before me, and I did not put away His statutes from me.*

*<sup>23</sup> I was also upright before Him, and I kept myself from mine iniquity.*

*<sup>24</sup> Therefore hath the LORD recompensed me according to my righteousness, according to the cleanness of my hands in His eyesight.*

The things you see, the pressure you feel, and the time between believing and receiving will try to contradict what God has already declared. This has been the case from the Bible days through today. Elijah declared to Ahab that rain was coming; six times, Elijah told his servant to go look for a sign of rain but he saw nothing (1 Kings 18:44).

## Developed Through Dirt

Moses went to Pharaoh ten times and was denied from even after God gave him the promise of deliverance for his people (Exodus 5-10). Jairus went to see Jesus when his daughter was sick and as he was on his way, she died (Mark 5:35). Lazarus died, was wrapped up and had started decomposing before Jesus responded to Mary and Martha's request (John 11). God gave the Shunamite woman the promise of a child yet her son died. God made Mary a promise of birthing the Savior but Mary didn't realize she, Joseph and baby Jesus would have to flee for their lives (Matthew 2:13). Years later, it looked like Mary's promise had completely died but Jesus' death and resurrection was all a part of a larger plan (Matthew 27).

Persistently staying in faith while problems seems to progress will lead to a standoff…the pressure versus the promise. One is going to give up. Which one is dependent on you and the actions you take. How you respond to the pressure is a major indicator of what's in you.

I'm sure we can all agree when I say problems seems to happen at the most inopportune time. Even Jesus experienced a highly pressurized "bad" day. In Mark 6, Jesus learned of the beheading of His beloved cousin John the Baptist. In the same span of time, the disciples had just returned from the mission field excited and anxious to share with Jesus all they had seen and done. In an attempt to regroup and decompress, Jesus instructed them to get away from the hustle and bustle of the days' activities. Jesus and the disciples could not leave fast enough before the throngs of people surrounded them. It was at this pressurized point when Jesus had a choice to either criticize and

## Perfected Through Pressure

check the people for invading His space and personal time or show compassion and minister to their needs, delaying His own need to grieve (remember, Jesus was a man who experienced emotions like us too). I can remember during the last moments of my grandmother's life, I received a message from someone needing prayer and encouragement. I told the person I was in hospice with my dying grandmother but that didn't seem to matter. I put aside my grieving (although I had a bit of an attitude) to minister to this person. From that incident, I began to understand Jesus' thoughts and feelings during that moment.

After Jesus ministered to the crowd, He then tells the disciples, who had just returned from running a miracle revival, where they saw signs and wonders manifest from their preached words, to feed the crowd of people. They saw Jesus' request as mission impossible. Up to this point, these men had first-hand accounts of the miraculous power of God to do the impossible yet they responded as if they were brand new to the operations of faith. Jesus could have EASILY and justifiably responded to them sternly but He used that pressure to produce miracles and turned it to yet another teachable moment.

When the pressure was on the disciples to feed the 5,000, they failed the test. Doubt clouded their faith in God to perform a miracle. The miracle was not solely to satisfy the immediate need of hunger. It was designed to point the people back to the Father. Jesus satisfied the soulish need so that the focus can be on the greater need of spiritual satisfaction.

## Developed Through Dirt

After feeding the 5,000 plus people, He sent His disciples away to rest and He went away to pray. He needed some alone time in the presence of God the Father. After His fellowship with the Father, Jesus proceeds to meet them on the other side, walking on the water and would have passed them up had they not yelled out in fear (verses 45-51). You see, Jesus had every intention of passing them up because He gave them instructions to meet Him on the other side. When Jesus instructed them to go to the other side, His instructions were filled with enough power and protection to get them there. Jesus will never tell you to do something and not provide the means and wherewithal for you to do it. Now remember, Jesus was in the same storm, yet He walked on the water in the midst of the storm. Just as He was not moved by the pressure of the storm but was pushing through it unphased, so too did He expect the disciples to do the same thing. Yet, once again, the pressures of the current situation made them respond in fear. In each of the pressurized situations, Jesus made a decision to rob the circumstance of any opportunity to cause Him to respond in fear or out of emotions.

The enemy will attempt to use pressure to make you react in the flesh, responding as if God is a non-existent factor in your life. Some years ago, I went to the doctor for my annual exam. The doctor had a look on his face that I did not like. He finally told me that he felt a lump in my breast and had ordered a mammogram. Fear immediately tried to seize me and the pressure was pushing me to respond negatively. Remember, first words are critical. If you are not saying what the Word says, confusion will set in. The grave danger in that is

## Perfected Through Pressure

confusion will lead to a standstill, resulting in no progress. No progress leads to stagnation. Stagnation leads to becoming lukewarm.

### *Revelations 5:15-17, 19* (MSG)

*15-17 "I know you inside and out, and find little to my liking. You're not cold, you're not hot—far better to be either cold or hot! You're stale. You're stagnant. You make me want to vomit. You brag, 'I'm rich, I've got it made, I need nothing from anyone,' oblivious that in fact you're a pitiful, blind beggar, threadbare and homeless.*

*19 "The people I love, I call to account—prod and correct and guide so that they'll live at their best. Up on your feet, then! About face! Run after God!*

I immediately said I was already healed and whole. After that, several healing scriptures came flooding out of my mouth. I refused to succumb to the pressure of an evil report. I did not receive it; instead, I had a peace (Isaiah 26:3) in knowing Jesus had provided healing for me on the Cross and I received the fullness of His work right then.

On the day of my mammogram, I went in fighting fear with the Word of God.

### *1 Peter 2:24*

*Who His own self bare our sins in His own body on the tree, that we, being dead to sins, should live unto righteousness: by whose stripes ye were healed.*

# Developed Through Dirt

*Matthew 8:17*

*That it might be fulfilled which was spoken by Esaias the prophet, saying, Himself took our infirmities and bare out sickness.*

*Isaiah 53:5*

*He was wounded for our transgressions, He was bruised for our iniquities: the chastisement of our peace was upon Him; and with His stripes we are healed.*

*Psalm 103:1-2*

*Bless the Lord, O my soul, and forget not all His benefits: Who forgiveth all thine iniquities; who healeth all thy diseases; who redeemeth thy life from destruction.*

Whenever a negative thought came, I confessed those scriptures. I had zero opportunities to entertain a negative thought.

After the x-rays were done, the technician left me in the machine just in case she needed another view. I looked at the monitor she was viewing and saw the mass. I looked at the mass and spoke my healing scriptures and declared I'm not moved by what I see; I'm already healed. She had to do a second set of x-rays and this time there was no mass. She searched and searched, twisted and turned me in various positions but nothing showed up on the x-rays. Frustrated, she

## Perfected Through Pressure

exclaimed, "I don't know what happened; it was just there a few moments ago." I thanked God immediately for His miraculous power because I knew it was Him responding to my faith. I had pressured my pressure and troubled my trouble! Paul said *"these light afflictions which are but for a moment..."* Romans 8 says *through faith and patience, the promise was manifested* (paraphrase).

Even though you know God made you a promise, pressure will try to force you to respond in fear or try to make it happen on your own. There are perilous risks in trying to make the promise of God come to pass on your own. We can learn from Abraham's experience of trying to expedite the promises of God on his own when the pressure of old age was moving him to doubt. When God told Abraham that he and Sarah would have a son, he became impatient in how long he was having to wait so they took matters into their own hands and produced Ishmael with Hagar. Because Abraham went ahead of God's timing, he caused chaos and dissention in their household. To this day, the Arab nation, which is a descendant of Ishmael, has been at odds with the Israeli nation. Disobedience will not only affect you but your family now and potentially generations to come.

Just as one act of obedience can change your life forever, so too can one act of disobedience have a lasting effect on your lineage. The proof is in the story….it's never solely about you. The pressure of waiting on the promise to manifest while steadily getting old showed what was really in Abraham. Sure he believed God but he did not trust God. Had he trusted God, he would not have taken matters into his own hands. The enemy will use time to pressure you to move outside of God's divine timetable.

Once you get in faith, stay in faith no matter how much time seems to stand still. Staying in faith will bring a rest, produces anticipation, and creates opportunities that otherwise would be non-existent. We can look at the woman with the issue of blood in Mark 5:25-34 (MSG):

> *25-29 A woman who had suffered a condition of hemorrhaging for twelve years—a long succession of physicians had treated her, and treated her badly, taking all her money and leaving her worse off than before—had heard about Jesus. She slipped in from behind and touched his robe. She was thinking to herself, "If I can put a finger on his robe, I can get well." The moment she did it, the flow of blood dried up. She could feel the change and knew her plague was over and done with. 30 At the same moment, Jesus felt energy discharging from him. He turned around to the crowd and asked, "Who touched my robe?" 31 His disciples said, "What are you talking about? With this crowd pushing and jostling you, you're asking, 'Who touched me?' Dozens have touched you!" 32-33 But he went on asking, looking around to see who had done it. The woman, knowing what had happened, knowing she was the one, stepped up in fear and trembling, knelt*

## Perfected Through Pressure

> *before him, and gave him the whole story. <sup>34</sup> Jesus said to her, "Daughter, you took a risk of faith, and now you're healed and whole. Live well, live blessed! Be healed of your plague."*

To the human senses, there was no way to have that one-on-one encounter with Jesus with all those people fighting to get touched by Him. Instead, she touched Him in faith, something others were not doing, otherwise they would have been healed like her. The woman exhausted every resource she had but there was no change in her situation. No matter what, her thought did not deviate…*if I could touch Him…* the "thought" mentioned in verse 28 means to repeatedly say, to meditate, which is a form of internal confession and profession.

### *Joshua 1:8b (TLB)*

> *<sup>8</sup> but thou shalt meditate therein day and night, that thou mayest observe to do according to all that is written therein: for then thou shalt make thy way prosperous, and then thou shalt have good success.*

### *Hebrews 10:23*

> *<sup>23</sup> Let us hold fast the profession of our faith without wavering; (for He is faithful that promised;)*

How desperate will you become for a change? Are you willing to go against "religious" protocol and touch Jesus? Are you willing to let go of inhibitions and reach for Him? Are you willing to let your worship be so passionate and heartfelt that it ruffles the feathers of others but touches the heart of God? Are you willing to abandon those around you and go after God with all that's in you and seize your moment? Or will you allow pressure to paralyze you?

This woman meditated on her healing so much that it built a confidence for her to break protocol, go in public and be in the presence of a Rabbi. This could have gotten her stoned to death but her faith in God superseded her fear of what they could do.

### *Hebrews 13:5-6* (MSG)

*[5-6] Since God assured us, "I'll never let you down, never walk off and leave you," we can boldly quote,*

*God is there, ready to help;*
*I'm fearless no matter what.*
*Who or what can get to me?*

What you are going through, the pressures you are under, the troubles you face is difficult. I get that. The path God has you on and what He's allowing in your life will not make sense most of the time but the developing of your faith is not for the normal, earthly, unrenewed mind. Did it make sense for Elisha to tell Naaman to dip seven times in filthy water (2 Kings 5)? Did it make sense to spit in mud and put the mixture on a blind man's eyes (John 9)? Did it make sense for Esther and the nation of Israel to go on a fast when a genocide was being planned against them (Esther 9)?

## Perfected Through Pressure

God's ways does not follow a natural course or pre-packaged pattern that flows with the "normal" way of being and doing. Faith will put you in a place of uncertainty but that uncertainty is not if God can do it. The uncertainty is really whether YOU can do it, whether YOU can handle it. I'll save you some time, YOU can't but God most certainly can.

# The Pain of the Process: Hurting But Not Hopeless

*2 Corinthians 4:17*
*For our light affliction, which is but for a moment,*
*worketh for us a far more exceeding*
*and eternal weight of glory.*

For several months after I was laid off, I had been battling severe allergies and hay fever. Perfect timing, as my insurance had just lapsed! Once I started working again, I made an appointment to see an Ear, Nose and Throat specialist. After running a battery of checks, he gave me a type of allergy test called the Scratch Test, which would help to get the precise diagnosis for what was ailing me. With the test, they put a small amount of allergen on my forearm but nothing happened. It was not until they used a needle to scratch my skin at each place where the allergen was located when I had a reaction. The irritation indicated what was in me causing a reaction.

The primary purpose of scratch test was never meant to hurt or harm me. It was very purposeful and strategic. The tests were hand-chosen and controlled. It didn't last long and there was a small amount used under the doctor's control to help expose potentially harmful allergens. The small exposure to the actual allergen was to prevent a huge reaction later on and possibly death. The doctor knew how long the discomfort would last. The test revealed internal build-up and toxicity within my system. The doctor caused the irritation but also provided the ointment to relieve the pain.

And so it goes in the Spirit. You never really know what's in you until irritants come to expose it. You may not realize what's lying dormant in you until a contrary situation "scratches" you. It was only after I got scratched that the doctor could see what the problem was and how to effectively treat it.

The test was completely uncomfortable and unexpected but totally essential if I was to become healthy. During that moment, it felt like my arm was on fire; there was an unexplainable itch and irritation that felt impossible to soothe. If left to my mind to tell the story, the discomfort and pain lasted a long time. In actuality, it was only an hour from the time he administered the test to the time the administered allergen lost its effectiveness.

You too have gone through or are currently in situations that are so horrendous, so painful, and so toxic that you don't think you'll survive. If you were like me, you had thoughts of "this test is going to take me out Lord. Where are you? This pain is intolerable. It hurts too much. Please get me out of this mess." Does any part of this sound familiar? Take comfort in knowing, this *scratch test* is but for a moment.

As painful of a situation you're facing, Jesus went through a much worse ordeal and experienced a pain that is beyond belief. Before you complain about the pain and about what you are facing is not fair, consider Jesus. Was it fair that He left His deity in Heaven to come to earth as a mere man? Was it fair that He left the grandeur of Heaven to endure the mediocrity of earth? Was it fair that He, who was perfect and sinless, took our sins and became the ultimate sacrifice for our wrongdoings? Was it fair that He was beaten without a cause? Was it fair that He was disrespected by those merciless soldiers? Was it fair that His mother had to see Him beaten and crucified? Was it fair that He was beaten beyond recognition? Was it fair that He was mocked and taunted by onlookers? Was it fair that Jesus died the most horrific, painful and public death ever created by man?

I'm in no way trying to minimize or dismiss what you are going through in life; I'm just asking you to keep the pain in perspective and consider Jesus. From the study Dr. William Edwards and his team conducted on the physical death of Jesus[1], consider our ultimate example:

- ❖ From the time of Jesus sweating drops of blood through the scourging on the following day (Good Friday as we call it), Jesus suffered horrific beatings at the hands of expert executioners, the Roman soldiers, a sleepless night, hunger, and in all of this, He was forced to walk more than 2.5 miles, travelling between the various trial sites.
- ❖ The whip used to beat Him was made of leather thongs which had iron balls, shards of glass, and sheep bones on its ends.
- ❖ The iron balls on the whip were strategically designed to cause deep bruises while the bones and glass would cut into the skin

## Hurting Not Hopeless

and tissues, eventually creating ribbons of flesh to hang off of His body.
- ❖ The severe blood loss and pain caused circulatory shock.
- ❖ A robe was placed on His shoulders and back and when the soldiers snatched the robe from Jesus' back, it is very probable that they reopened the fresh wounds that had begun to clot.
- ❖ They placed a crown of thorns on His head and had beaten His head and crown with a wooden staff, driving the thorns deeper into His scalp, piercing both the skin and scalp and causing more hemorrhaging.
- ❖ The soldiers strapped the 100-pound cross beam to His shoulders, which were bleeding profusely and had ripples of tissue and muscle now barely attached to His body.
- ❖ Between the scourging, the excessive blood loss, shock, pain, extreme exhaustion and dehydration, He had no strength to carry the Cross very far. His body had been pushed well beyond the highest level of endurance, so He fell to the ground, with the 100-pound weight falling on top of Him, further ripping His flesh, contaminating it with dirt and bugs, and causing radiating pain to shoot through His entire body.
- ❖ Nails, which were actually iron spikes that were between 5 and 7 inches long with a 3/8" square shaft, were driven through His hands (wrist) and feet, cutting major arteries and nerves, causing excruciating and fiery bolts of pain to radiate through His body with each breath He took, eventually causing paralysis of a portion of His hands.

## Developed Through Dirt

- ❖ It was painfully difficult just to take shallow breaths, which was what His respiratory function had been reduced to at that point. To exhale and inhale, Jesus had to push down on the nails in His feet to raise His body and allow His rib cage to move downwards and inwards to expire air from His lungs, which meant scraping His raw, flesh beaten back against the rugged Cross.
- ❖ Because of fluctuating oxygen levels, Jesus' heart and pulse rate increased exponentially; eventually His heart began to fail.

In addition to the physical pain, Jesus endured a spiritual pain that far supersedes the physical anguish He endured. He cried out *"My God, My God why hast Thou forsaken Me"* (Matthew 27:46). Have you ever been in a relationship where the two of you were inseparable and deeply in love? Then one day something happened that caused you two to break up and part ways. Do you recall the deep hurt, pain, endless tears, and how you wanted it all to go away? Well intensify that by a zillion or the highest conceivable number and you will BEGIN to have an idea of the separation anxiety Jesus experienced when He took on the whole of humanity's sin, past, present and future. Not even factoring in His habitation in Heaven, for 33 years while on earth, Jesus was in constant contact with the Father. SEVERAL times He talked about His relationship with the Father:

## Hurting Not Hopeless

***John 14:9-11*** *-* [9] *Jesus replied, "Don't you even yet know who I am, Philip, even after all this time I have been with you? Anyone who has seen Me has seen the Father! So why are you asking to see Him?*[10] *Don't you believe that I am in the Father and the Father is in Me? The words I say are not My own but are from My Father who lives in Me. And He does His work through Me.* [11] *Just believe it—that I am in the Father and the Father is in Me.*

***John 12:49*** *- I don't speak on My own authority. The Father who sent Me has commanded Me what to say and how to say it.*

***John 5:19*** *(ESV) - So Jesus said to them, "Truly, truly, I say to you, the Son can do nothing of His own accord, but only what He sees the Father doing. For whatever the Father does, that the Son does likewise.*

***John 17:21*** *(TLB) - I pray that they will all be one, just as You and I are one--as You are in Me, Father, and I am in You. And may they be in Us so that the world will believe You sent Me.*

***John 10:30*** *- I and My Father are one.*

To go from being one with the Father to being the epitome of sin was drastic, dramatic and extremely hard because it brought a separation between Him and the Father. Just as a baby cries when they realize their parent is gone and when a person cries when they part ways with their significant other/mate, so too did Jesus cry out *"ELI, ELI, LAMA SABACHTHANI?" that is, "MY GOD, MY GOD, WHY HAVE YOU FORSAKEN ME?"* (Matthew 27:46).

From an emotional and social perspective, so great was the stress, strain and pressure in just thinking about what He was to endure that tiny capillaries in Jesus' head broke and caused Him to sweat blood (Luke 22:44). The disciples, who were with Jesus more than His family was for those last three years, had all abandoned Him upon His arrest in the Garden of Gethsemane (Mark 14:50). Peter, one of the chief apostles, denied Jesus on multiple occasions (Luke 22:54-62). Jesus was naked when He was beaten and crucified (the traditional way Romans crucified people), publically exposing Him to all those who were there, including the mother of our Lord, along with the other women. Jesus was falsely accused, jeered, spat upon and then died a criminal's death, which was the most shameful way to die during that era, as it was reserved for the vilest criminals and "scum of the earth."

The scripture tells us that Jesus is touched with the feelings of our infirmities (Hebrews 4:15) and experienced all of our pain ahead of us. No matter what pain you are experiencing, Jesus' pain was infinitely more than human comprehension so the next time you feel it's too much to bear, your pain is more than you can stand, consider Jesus!

Had Jesus been immediately removed from His horrific ordeal of betrayal, beating and death, Scripture would not have been fulfilled and our redemption would not have been made possible. The bigger plan would have been short-circuited to relieve His momentary anguish, albeit great anguish it was. In His moments of agony when He cried out in the Garden of Gethsemane, the Father didn't take Him out of the time of testing He was about to endure. What God did was strengthen Jesus to go through it all; He was strengthened to die.

Because Jesus faced and conquered the Cross, we don't have to bear the full burden of our trials. To be truthful, we really don't experience the totality of what we should be experiencing. It's only because of His grace and mercy that we don't face the fullness of what we deserve or the full extent of what the devil wants to inflict. If God really gave us what we deserved, we wouldn't be able to take it. Jesus bore the worst of it for us. That's enough to pause and praise Him right now!

God had a purpose in allowing Jesus to endure such suffering. He saw all of us being reunited back to Himself, restoring us back to the Garden of Eden experience. Can you imagine the greatest family reunion ever, where there is a continuous habitation and unrestricted access to the presence of God Almighty with an unending supply of love, peace, joy, and provision? Also, because Jesus knew it would please the Father, He gladly accepted the path of pressure and pain, knowing the final outcome would be joy forevermore.

***Hebrews 12:2**  – For the joy set before Him, He endured the Cross.*

## Developed Through Dirt

It is very easy to question God while suffering: God where are You while I am going through this divorce? Where are You while I raise these three kids by myself? Where are You while I try to figure out where the money is going to come from to pay my mortgage, which is now four months behind? Where were you when I had to bury my father while dealing with my wife cheating on me? Where were You when I was being raped? Where were You when my daughter was murdered? Where were You when I had to drop out of school because I had no financial aid? Why would you allow me to have a miscarriage? Where were you when I lost my job? Where were You when I was alone and abandoned as my uncles molested me and then my grandmother gave me up for adoption…WHERE WERE YOU? WHY DID THIS HAPPEN?

He understands the hurt you have endured and the emotional and physical scars the battles have left behind. He has heard every prayer you've prayed and captured every tear you've cried. He sees all. He hears all. He knows all. He feels all. This is why I can confidently say *"all things work together for the good* (Romans 8:28)." No it doesn't feel, look, or seem good, but God is masterfully crafting every experience into something that will be good as well as bring honor and glory to Him, will bring help and healing to people and will bring hope and happiness to you.

What are you to do with those broken and dark pieces of your life that doesn't seem to be any good? Hand it to God and watch Him perform the ultimate makeover from what you deemed as irreparable!

## Hurting Not Hopeless

If you leave those broken pieces untreated and in its current state with all their sharp, jagged edges, they will remain a hazard and threat to your life, causing cuts, bruises, and discomfort not only to yourself but others around you. If the cut is deep enough, it can potentially cause hemorrhaging.

When you look at a mosaic art piece, it is a rare and beautiful work of fine art. Although the beauty shines through the artwork, the true beauty is knowing that the mosaic was crafted and designed using broken pieces. Life has dealt some lethal blows to you that caused you to be broken into many pieces but you have been broken in the right places. These broken pieces of your life are not useless, neither should you look at yourself nor the lot of what you've experienced as worthless; it will all be repurposed for a greater use. God can and will make each of those broken pieces fit perfectly together and will then put you on display as a work of art. When God sees you, He does not see a sum total of broken pieces; He sees you as a masterpiece that is unique, beautiful and fit for purpose.

Even in the process of making mosaics, there is some chiseling away, chipping, cutting and reshaping to make the pieces fit. Romans 8:18 tells us that *"our present sufferings are not worth comparing with the glory that will be revealed in us."*

# Buried Alive

*John 12:24*
*Except a corn of wheat fall into the ground and die, it abideth alone: but if it die, it bringeth forth much fruit.*

I must confess I had a huge challenge when I read John 12:24...*unless the grain falls to the ground and die*. I've read this scripture plenty of times but it's something about reading it at that particular moment that struck a chord in me. This was right before the series of challenges came to greet me! My spirit was trying to prepare me and my flesh had already begun to cry out before any sign of changes happened.

I felt I had gone through enough, as I had already fought a trilogy of wars: my mom battling cancer, my nephew fighting for his life after having been crushed by a van, and the turmoil on my job. Surely this was enough to last a lifetime but deep down I knew there was more to come for the sake of the call of God on my life. For the purpose to which I was called, I discerned there was a greater sacrifice and development that was required. Did I have a choice....sure! I could have taken the path of least resistance but I would not experience the fullness of joy, peace and satisfaction in knowing I have done the perfect will of the Father for my life.

## Buried Alive

Once again, God was using nature to speak to me. He was showing me that a seed is not purposed and designed to remain a seed. A seed is created specifically for the purpose of producing a harvest AND more seed so it is necessary to bury the seed and leave it underground for a season. Great things happen while underground….the roots are forming, the internal structure is being developed, and the support system is being established for the plant. Everything that the plant/tree will ever become is already pre-coded inside the seed but until the seed is buried, broken and exposed, the true value is not realized and the true purpose cannot be produced. In other words, get comfortable with being uncomfortable!

I read about Paul and David and Joseph and Abraham and Jesus. Each time I read about these men of faith, my spirit bore witness and identified with their lives. I have always been extremely blessed and ministered to by the revelations and truths the Apostle Paul shared in his books, especially in the book in Philippians, which was written while he was in a Roman prison. He was constantly chained, literally 24/7, to a prison guard. Apparently they heard about the Paul and Silas jail experience (Acts 16:24–40) and heard about Peter's experience (Acts 12: 5–17) and did not want a repeat of embarrassment.

At this point, Paul had been in jail for four years. Prior to that, Paul was shipwrecked, bitten by a poisonous snake, nearly stoned to death, beaten several times, nearly drowned yet, he *counted it all joy* and said *"that I may know Him in the fellowship of His suffering….*(Philippians 3:10)." Joy doesn't mean that you are happy with all the circumstances. It doesn't mean that your circumstances are what you would choose or that you have control over them. It means that in the midst of the trials, you have something that will bring you through it. You have an inner knowing that trouble won't last always. You have a confidence of this very thing...*He which has begun a good work in you is faithful to complete it* (Philippians 1:6). In the midst of a prison sentence, Paul wrote, *Rejoice in the Lord always and again I say REJOICE* (Philippians 4:4). Some of the most quoted New Testament scriptures are from the book of Philippians:

### *Philippians 2:13-15*

> *For it is God which worketh in you both to will and to do of His good pleasure. Do all things without murmuring and disputings: that ye may be blameless and harmless, the sons of God, without rebuke, in the midst of a crooked and perverse nation, among whom ye shine as lights in the world.*

### *Philippians 3:8-9a, 10*

> *I count all things but loss for the excellency of the knowledge of Christ Jesus my Lord: for whom I have suffered the loss of all things and do count them but dung that I may win Christ and be found in Him. That I may know Him and the power of His resurrection, and the fellowship of His suffering, being made conformable unto His death;*

# Buried Alive

### *Philippians 3:13-14*

*I count not myself to have apprehended; but this one thing I do, forgetting those things which are behind, and reaching forth unto those things which are before, I press toward the mark for the prize of the high calling of God in Christ Jesus.*

### *Philippians 4:4*

*Rejoice in the Lord always and again I say Rejoice.*

### *Philippians 4:6*

*Be careful for nothing; but in everything by prayer and supplication with thanksgiving let your requests be made known unto God. And the peace of God which passeth all understanding shall keep your hearts and minds through Christ Jesus. Finally brethren whatsoever things are true, whatsoever things are honest, whatsoever things are just, whatsoever things are pure, whatsoever things are lovely, whatsoever things are of good report; if there be any virtue, and if there be any praise, think on these things.*

### *Philippians 4:13*

*I can do all things through Christ which strengtheneth me.*

## Developed Through Dirt

### *Philippians 4:19*

*But my God shall supply all your need according to His riches in glory by Christ Jesus.*

Inspite of false imprisonment, false accusations, and persecutions from his fellow laborers in the gospel, it takes great maturity to say, *"WHAT HAS HAPPENED TO ME HAS REALLY SERVED TO ADVANCE THE GOSPEL* (Philippians 1:12)." While in prison, his focus and fix was on ministering to others. While in his isolation and horrid conditions, he was encouraging and instructing the Church.

I didn't realize some of these very words would be what I needed to cling to during the storms of life. At one point, I literally felt buried by all the tests, troubles, challenges, pain and situations I encountered. One of the worst feelings one can experience is that of being buried. However, this type of "burial" is needful and rewarding because the end results will be much more than you expected; have faith and know that the process is unearthing the pre-coded destiny in you.

My greatest fight during my "burial process" was not against the enemy. My two greatest fights were between my head and my heart to trust God enough to release it all to Him and rest in His promises. I was being developed not destroyed. The Holy Spirit began to minister to me and really challenged my faith. He asked:

- ❖ Can you trust Me when your flesh is crying out for relief?

## Buried Alive

- Can you trust Me past your feelings of mistrust and doubt towards others?
- Can you trust Me when others seem to fail you?
- Can you trust Me when family turn on you?
- Can you trust Me when your job has been eliminated?
- Can you trust Me when you don't feel loved?
- Can you trust Me when you don't know what your next move will be?
- Can you trust Me when you don't see a clear path?
- Can you trust Me when don't see a way at all?
- Can you trust Me after you lose everything?
- Can you trust Me while in pain?
- Can you trust Me when all seems hopeless?
- Can you believe Me to deliver you?
- Can you love beyond your emotions…..love beyond your pain…..love beyond what's easy and convenient?
- Can you love those who mistreat you?
- Can you love those who lie on you?
- Can you love the unlovable?

The challenge was a bit jarring because I wanted to take the self-protective stance… "but what about them…" I had BROKEN FOCUS! He couldn't use me to the extent that He wanted to with me still being PETTY. I had to die to that kind of thinking.

After laughing and then evaluating my actions, I needed the burial process more than I realized. God had a real sense of humor and

## Developed Through Dirt

a loving way of correcting me. He said "You're not dead yet (remember, unless a kernel of wheat falls into the ground and die…). You're dying but still have reflexes, still trying to talk, still attempting to run, like it's a movie scene. Completely die until you decompose and the former you does not exist anymore. When you are completely decomposed, you will become a nutrient-rich substance to produce growth to things all around you."

I had to face the harsh reality that I was not enduring hardness (of being buried) *as a good soldier* like Paul instructed in 2 Timothy 2:3. A good soldier is a follower of his commander. A good soldier is faithful to the mission and assignment given, even if he doesn't like it or agree with it. He takes the orders and then goes and execute them until the mission is accomplished; to not do so is considered treason. A good soldier is equipped for the mission and is skilled in using his tools. A good soldier is determined to be honorable and avoid actions that will disgrace his unit, his superior and ultimately his country. A good soldier spends time getting strategies from the commanding officer. He studies the methods of his enemy and learns his weaknesses and then exploit them to the fullest extent of his ability. A good soldier not only cares about his own welfare, but he also looks out for the welfare of his fellow soldiers. A good soldier does not retreat in the face of the enemy; he does not run from a fight. Instead, he stands his ground and fights the battle until the battle is over; he does not quit at the first hint of trouble. A good soldier realizes that the battle does not run according to his time frame; he knows that another is in charge of the duration of the battle. A good soldier is in the battle to the finish.

## Buried Alive

A good soldier dedicates himself to keeping his oath. A good soldier knows it's ok to cry but knows, at some point, he must dry the tears and keep pressing forward.

To further see the tactics and dynamics of an excellent soldier, I began to study them. As a lover of history, I was really intrigued by a British general by the name of Arthur Duke Wellington. He was credited with leading his army to defeat Napoleon at Waterloo. The Duke had to overcome many setbacks, including his own mother's lack of faith in him, in order to make a success of his military career. She once commented: "I vow to God I don't know what I shall do with my awkward son, Arthur[1]." She even believed he had little aptitude for soldiering! Perhaps this motivated him to become one of the greatest generals in British military history. From an early age, many people are programmed by their own parents and friends who place verbal limits on what they can achieve. Too often, they allow these limits to control them for the rest of their lives. Wellesley, for one, managed to demolish the limits placed on him by his mother.

In 1808, he arrived in Portugal, which was occupied by the French who had seemed unbeatable to everyone. Wellesley told a friend that he would not be chased off the continent as so many other similar forces had been; he was not afraid of them as everybody else seemed to be. Wellington knew how to stand steady in the face of a fearsome attack and he instilled the same spirit into his troops.

Being calm, cool, collected and courageous are major factors in most victory stories. Too many people are beaten by their own lack of self-confidence before they even start. If they do start and run into problems, they panic, which can quickly lead to failure because your mind is not clear and levelled enough to make quality decisions.

The Duke was not a man to be dominated or threatened by anyone. He was a man of action and few words; he planned very carefully and took great care to choose the right ground for his battles. Success demands both planning and action.

When asked for his formula of success for the then most powerful army in the world, Duke Wellington said the success is simple: the British army is able to fight five minutes longer than any enemy[2]. That is the key to being a spiritual champion. It is not always about being the most talented, the most affluent, or the most gifted. It is the person who will not give up, who will not give in to discouragement, who keeps on keeping on until the end.

*Matthew 24:13*

[13] But those enduring to the end shall be saved.

# Familial Dirt: The Promise, the Pit, the Prison, the Palace

*Romans 8:28*
*And we know all things work together for good*
*to them that love God, to them who are the called according to his*
*purpose.*

While in the thick of my dirt and development, the Word of God not only became my tool to fight but to also help me understand where I was and where I was headed. There are many men and women throughout the Bible who went through tragedy to get to the triumphant times in their lives yet none stick out to me like the story of Joseph. All the dirt heaped upon Joseph by family and those in authority over him helped him develop into the leader I so admire. Genesis 37 through 41 has always blessed me tremendously but it was not until recently that I saw the similarities between Joseph and Jesus and realized I was merely being pointed back to Christ.

- ❖ Both Joseph and Jesus were shepherds.
- ❖ Both were betrayed and sold out by Judas. You may say wait, Judah was the one to sell Joseph. You are correct. In Greek, Judah means Judas!
- ❖ Both were well-loved by their fathers.

## Developed Through Dirt

- ❖ Both were despised by their brothers.
- ❖ Both did not try to defend themselves when brought before the presiding ruler.
- ❖ Both were stripped of their garments....Joseph's coat and Jesus' robe.
- ❖ Both started their public ministry at the age of 30.

It was evident that the hand of God was on Joseph's life. His father knew something was special about this son and gave him preferential treatment over his siblings (Genesis 37:3), which caused problems, even eventually with his father. That favor factor had Joseph's brothers despising him and Joseph did not help this in any way when Joseph prematurely shared his destiny dream with his brothers, who Joseph KNEW did not like him. Ok I can chalk that up to immaturity. He was excited about what God was going to do. I get it...been there, done that. **HOWEVER,** inspite of his brothers' disdain for the first dream, he decided to share the SECOND dream with them, as if that was a great idea! Bad decision Joe Joe, BAD decision! Now his dream caused everyone in the family to be livid and at this point, even poppa Jacob is hotter than burnt fish grease. To me, that showed signs of arrogance and pride peering into Joseph's character.

Joseph's actions teach us a pivotal lesson: the favor of God will promote you and make you preferred over others but don't allow pride to puff you up and give you a false immunization to humility. There is a great responsibility of humbleness, respect, and gratitude

## The Promise, Pit, Prison, Palace

that comes with the favor of God. Let's not get it twisted....favor and grace are sheer gifts from God that did not warrant any activity from you to be a recipient of it. Remember, it's not really about you. Just as God had a plan that involved using Joseph as an earthly facilitator, so too does He have a plan that involves you. As I've said before, God's plan and purpose is much bigger than you. The blessings and benefits are the by-products of the plan and not the ultimate end product of the plan!

At times, uncommon favor is needed to usher you into a place and position that you otherwise couldn't qualify for or get to on your own merits or in a shorter span of time; God is positioning you for a purpose outside of just you. His plan requires you to be in a certain place at a certain time so His favor will escort you to where you need to be.

Isn't it amazing how some people will despise you because of the plan God has for you? They don't even know the full details and thank God for that because they are choking off the glimpse of what they can perceive. This was the case for Joseph. His brothers discerned something was different but they couldn't pinpoint it. They just knew God was with him. This was enough to drive them to a hatred and anger that contemplated killing their brother (Genesis 37:20). That spirit of jealousy took them to a place that I'm sure they did not want to go, which was murder. When you yield yourself to an evil influence, you cannot dictate how far it can take you. At that point, you no longer have jurisdictional authority to say what is permissible. You have willingly allowed the enemy a foothold in your thoughts and of course he will not stop there; he's going for full access, which is evident in what Joseph's brothers wanted to do. Not only were they going to murder him but also throw his dead corpse into a pit, hiding all evidence of his existence; they literally wanted to wipe his memory off the face of the earth. The enemy doesn't care who he uses to take you out before you fulfill your destiny, but using a family member or someone close to you is a sick added bonus for him.

While in your pit, there are pitfalls that you want to avoid so that your time there won't be prolonged: complaining, bitterness, selfishness (remember, it's truly not about you), plans for revenge, deep depression, despair, and resentment. Don't focus on the pit (problem) but use the pit as an incubator to cultivate an attitude of praise. Cultivate an appetite for His Word. Cultivate an awareness of His presence. Cultivate a mindset to see God in your situation. The first response may not be to do those things, but the more you suppress the flesh and praise God, the more you cultivate the proper attitude while in the pit. As a child (and even some adults), you don't start off wanting to eat fruits and vegetables but the more you eat it, the more the appetite for it will be cultivated.

While in the pit, Joseph had every opportunity and natural justification to be bitter. There is no worse hurt than hurt done by the hands of those closest to you, those who are supposed to love and support you. His family, people who shared the same DNA with him, turned on him. I'm sure thoughts of hatred, malice, ill-will and at

## The Promise, Pit, Prison, Palace

minimum revenge, maybe even murder surged through Joseph's mind and more than once. He was thrown into a pit (a place of isolation, a dark, dirty place, a place of desecration and destitution) by people who claimed to love him, look out for him and have his best interest in mind. This is the type of betrayal that will have you plotting ways of seeking revenge, making them hurt, not as much but even more than how they hurt you. On what I imagine was one of the worst days of his life, Joseph did not curse his brothers or God for allowing this to happen. Little did he know, the turmoil that he endured was preparation for where God was taking him.

Although satan desired to kill Joseph, the plan and hand of the Lord prevailed. Instead of killing him, the brothers sold him to some Ishmaelites. This may have seemed like a better option, but the mental anguish that Joseph went through previously was just as bad in this situation. Think about it....Ishmael was the cast away child of Abraham; Ishmael was scorned and rejected by Sarah and would not share in the fullness of the Abrahamic inheritance. *Ishmael's hand would be against everyone and he will live in hostility toward all his brothers* (Genesis 16:12), so there was a natural root of bitterness there. Do you not think that hostility would have continued with the following generations? OF COURSE! After facing attempted murder at the hands of his brothers, now Joseph had to wonder if his distant relatives would exact revenge on him. Would they torture and kill him?

## Developed Through Dirt

Once again, God's protection and favor was working for Joseph. Instead of vigilante justice from the Ishmaelites, they sold Joseph as a slave to Potiphar, a high-ranking Egyptian authority. You may think, ok despite being a slave, at least he's alive. True, *however*, there was much animosity between the Hebrews and Egyptians during that time and Joseph has now been sold to one of his people's greatest enemies.

The typical treatment of a slave is deplorable and dehumanizing YET God provided not only grace to endure every trial and test Joseph faced but also God superimposed His favor over the slave status and shielded him from being treated like a slave. Instead of being condemned to a life of harsh labor, Joseph was put in Potiphar's house to serve. The favor and plan of God superseded the enemy's plans. Joseph, the enslaved foreigner, was given the high ranking position of being second in command in a strange land. This also speaks of Joseph's intellectual aptitude and adaptability. God gifted him to not only learn the language and culture of a foreign place but became so proficient at it that he advanced to a place of power and authority in Potiphar's house. Although he was labeled as a slave, he did not conduct himself as one. Like Joseph, we must learn to not allow our current circumstances define who we truly are. There is more than meets the eye so don't let a temporary situation permanently label you.

God was at work all along during each and every situation Joseph encountered. He continued to bless and promote Joseph and

## The Promise, Pit, Prison, Palace

Joseph continued to honor and serve God while in the midst of the storm of advances from Potiphar's wife. Keep in mind, during this time, Joseph was a young, handsome, virile man and Potiphar's wife saw that. She made no qualms about making her intentions known to Joseph, but he resisted.

### *Genesis 39:9*

*How can I do a wicked thing as this? It would be a great sin against God.*

So even in a foreign land, Joseph still honored God despite the many opportunities to be bitter, including anger towards God for allowing this to happen to him. He could have completely embraced and immersed himself into the Egyptian culture since they were treating him, a slave, much better than his family, his blood, ever did.

Joseph's good life in the palace would soon end because of false accusations. Due to the trumped up charges made by Potiphar's lying, scheming, cheating, disloyal wife, Joseph was thrown into prison. Need I remind you of Potiphar's title? CHIEF EXECUTIONER! Joseph could have been killed by Potiphar but God's plan and protection is much bigger than any title or position! Even while thrown in prison, God's hand was on Joseph.

### Genesis 39:21 – 23 NLT

*²¹ But the LORD was with Joseph in the prison and showed him His faithful love. And the LORD made*

## Developed Through Dirt

*Joseph a favorite with the prison warden. <sup>22</sup> Before long, the warden put Joseph in charge of all the other prisoners and over everything that happened in the prison. <sup>23</sup> The warden had no more worries, because Joseph took care of everything. The LORD was with him and caused everything he did to succeed.*

While going through his experiences, Joseph was being developed and matured. He did not complain about all the injustices he suffered. The only time Joseph mentioned he maladies was when he told the baker to remember him once he gets out of prison and tell Pharaoh of all the injustices done to him.

While in prison, the baker and wine taster both had dreams that disturbed them. Joseph saw their troubled countenance and asked the baker and wine taster why were they sad. I imagine the response went something like this: "HELLO?! This is prison. What kind of foolish question is that? I didn't do anything wrong (as most people in prison say AND believe). I'm going to spend my last days in the wretched place. I have no family around; I've been rejected by the king. I no longer eat the choicest foods and drink the best wines. I went from having the best to being subjected to the absolute worst. So Joseph, think about that question and ask me again why I'm sad." Yet this simple question speaks volumes to the heart and character of Joseph. He may have been in prison, but his heart and mind was not imprisoned.

## The Promise, Pit, Prison, Palace

The baker and wine taster asked Joseph to interpret their dreams. Isn't it funny how the very thing that got Joseph in trouble (talking about dreams) was the very thing that facilitated his deliverance? The difference...timing, maturity and discernment! Joseph showed much humility and reliance on God when he said, *"Interpreting dreams is God's business" (Genesis 40:8 TLB)*. Even in an adverse place and under contrary conditions, your gifts will still work and ultimately shift the atmosphere. God will allow us to enter trials as covert operations to bring God into that place. As my pastor tells us, God will purposely put us in hostile places to manifest the Kingdom.

God's gifts and plan for Joseph's life was in full swing. The stage is set. BOOM! The manifestation of what Joseph told them has happened. I'm sure he was just as excited as the wine taster (not so much the baker)! I can hear Joseph say: 'Finally, this is it. I'm getting out of here because ole boy the wine taster is going to hook me up with Pharaoh, since I told him the interpretation God had given me.'

As you know, that was not the case at all. Two years...730 days...17,520 hours...1,051,200 minutes...63,072,000 seconds had passed. News flash...God's timing may not exactly sync up with your calendar but at His command, everything and everyone will fall into perfect alignment.

When Pharaoh had a dream no one could interpret, the wine taster stopped sipping long enough to remember Joseph. They sent for Joseph to interpret Pharaoh's dreams, at which time he was in the

## Developed Through Dirt

dungeon. Now remember when he was first put in, he was in prison. Before it was all said and done, Joseph was called out of the dungeon. This is the deepest, darkest part of the prison. Sometimes it may get even worse before your deliverance comes.

When Joseph got before Pharaoh, he did not try to hide his faith. As embittered as the Egyptians were with the Hebrews, Joseph **BOLDLY** proclaimed *"I can't do it by myself, but God will tell you what it means" Gen 41:16 (TLB)*. After God revealed the interpretation through Joseph, Pharaoh had put him in charge, making Joseph second in command. This promotion accelerated him beyond everyone, including Potiphar. He is now over the one who imprisoned him. The true test of character came when Joseph assumed his office and possessed power and authority in this new position. Mercy, kindness, prudence and wisdom was ingrained in Joseph's character while he went through his trials. This is evidenced by Joseph not exacting revenge on his brothers, Potiphar or anyone else who had wronged him. With great power comes great responsibility. Throughout all of this, God, the great strategist He is, was orchestrating every move in His plan. Step by step, God directed Joseph to his destination.

The seven years of harvest that Joseph had amassed was then sold to the world during the seven years of famine. When financial means were no longer sufficient, people began to offer whatever that had. This resulted in Joseph collecting all this wealth for Pharaoh, making him the premier empire. Pharaoh thought that was his wealth but he was just a safe for them until it was time for the release when

## The Promise, Pit, Prison, Palace

the Israelites made their massive exodus from Egypt. Seven years of global domination was a covert operation in which God was strategically positioning Joseph's people for possession. God allowed Joseph to orchestrate the biggest breakthrough the Israelites would have seen at that time. I'm sure Joseph hadn't realized that God was using him to set up his people, the Israelites, to have a massive accumulation of wealth when they departed Egypt.

It was purposed that Israel be in Egypt. God prospered and favored them tremendously but that was not their final destination. God didn't allow them to get completely comfortable. He had another place for them….a land of their own. To get to the promise God made Abraham, Joseph had to go through the pit and the prison.

# Rich Dirt Bountiful Harvest

*James 1:2-4*
*Consider it pure joy, my brothers and sisters, whenever you face trials of many kinds, <sup>3</sup> because you know that the testing of your faith produces perseverance.*
*<sup>4</sup> Let perseverance finish its work so that you may be mature and complete, not lacking anything.*

The very things that caused you the most angst will be your greatest testimony and opportunity to help others; your experiences are not for naught. What you cried about will be the same thing you will shout about in the future. Yes it hurt and you wondered why all the disaster, trouble, pain, trials, and tribulations happened to you, but it was all a part of God's design to mature you, develop character and cultivate an appetite for His plan, which is much bigger and spans beyond you and your plan. These situations enriched the dirt you were in during development to help produce a bountiful harvest.

By now you have come to realize crying, kicking, screaming and begging does not get you out of life's storms. Being a good person does not exempt you from facing difficulties. Your salvation does not insulate you from times of testing and trials. God is more interested in building your character more than making you comfortable. The Word says *in*

## Rich Dirt, Bountiful Harvest

*this world you **WILL** have tribulation and trials and distress and frustration; but be of good cheer, take courage; be confident, certain, undaunted, for I have overcome the world, I have deprived it of power to harm you and have conquered it for you (*John 16:33 Amp*)*. God then further confirms and guarantees the victory in 1 John 5:4 when He said *"For whatsoever is born of God overcometh the world; and this is the victory that overcometh the world, even our faith."*

Where you are now is not an indicator of where you will be. I, like many of you, want the end results, want the life of sweet success, or at least want a reprieve from the warfare. I will raise both hands and feet for this vote! To get that bountiful harvest, there's a process that cannot be circumvented. The perseverance of training, the perseverance of discipline, and the perseverance of practice will produce results that will remain far beyond your capacity to imagine it.

It is very tempting to ask God WHEN....When will this test be done? When will I be free of pain? When will the manifestation of my faith happen? When will my family finally get right and stay right? When will my mate come? When will I be done with these student loans? WHEN GOD WHEN? How long will I have to live from pay check to pay check? How long will I have to suffer with pain? How long will I have to deal with rebellious children? How long will I have to suffer in silence? How long....not long!

## Developed Through Dirt

You will have to fight to keep the faith, especially when you've done everything you know how to do. You keep speaking faith, you remain positive when nothing but negativity hits you from the north, south, east and west. You faithfully tithe and give, even when you don't have money left after you give. You continue to walk in love and forgive, even when people treat you wrong, unjustly accuse you and speak unfavorably of you. You walk away from an argument when you really want to beat the brakes off the person. You don't respond in anger when your boss comes at you incorrectly. You continue to love and respect your spouse when their behavior does not reflect the same sentiment. You are sowing all of these good seeds yet you see no return for your investments; the harvest has not yet manifested. You fight the thought and attitude of "what's the use in doing right, living right and being right. It gets me nowhere." Your patience is growing thin, your faith is being stretched to the max. Your grip seems to be loosening. My brother, my sister, don't give up. Don't quit. You are closer than you realize.

### *Galatians 6:9 (NLT)*

> *So let's not get tired of doing what is good. At just the right time we will reap a harvest of blessing if we don't give up.*

Breakthrough <u>will</u> come. You could very well be days, hours, minutes or seconds from your breakthrough and harvest. Just as birthing pains from labor are the most intense right before delivery, so too is the intensity of your trials the worst right before the breakthrough. Don't give up!

I admit that during your testing season, one of the greatest challenges is waiting. Habakkuk 2:3 (TLB) tells us *"These things I plan won't happen right away, slowly, steadily, surely the time approaches when the vision will be fulfilled. If it seems slow do not despair for these things will surely come to pass. Just be patient – they will not be overdue a single day."* In the book of James, a perfect comparison is given of how farming principles mirror spiritual principles:

> *⁷ See how the farmer waits for the land to yield its valuable crop, patiently waiting for the autumn and spring rains. ⁸ You too, be patient and stand firm.*

You don't know the length of time between your declaration of faith, your dream, your vision, your goal and the fruition of it, but God has supplied you with many promises and guarantees that the vision and dream will be fulfilled to help fortify your faith during the wait.

### *1 John 5:15-15 (Amp)*

> *¹⁴ And this is the confidence (the assurance, the privilege of boldness) which we have in Him: [we are sure] that if we ask anything (make any request) according to His will (in agreement with His own plan), He listens to and hears us. ¹⁵ And if (since) we [positively] know that He listens to*

*us in whatever we ask, we also know [with settled and absolute knowledge] that we have [granted us as our present possessions] the requests made of Him.*

### *Romans 8:26-28*

*Meanwhile, the moment we get tired in the waiting, God's Spirit is right alongside helping us along. If we don't know how or what to pray, it doesn't matter. He does our praying in and for us, making prayer out of our wordless sighs, our aching groans. He knows us far better than we know ourselves, knows our pregnant condition, and keeps us present before God. That's why we can be so sure that every detail in our lives of love for God is worked into something good.*

### *Matthew 24:35*

*Heaven earth will pass away but My Words will never disappear.*

### *2 Corinthians 2:14*

*Thanks be unto God who always causes us to triumph.*

### *Romans 8:37 (NLT)*

*Despite all these things, overwhelming victory is ours through Christ, who loved us.*

### Rich Dirt, Bountiful Harvest

Time may try to dictate to you that nothing is happening. There may not be any outward signs of change but keep confessing your desired end; at the right time, all will be revealed. In Job 22, it says *"decree a thing and it shall be established."* Change *is* happening. Harvest *is* coming. When Jesus cursed the fig tree in Matthew 21, there was no evidence that what He spoken had manifested, yet the moment He spoke, change began to take place from the inside and eventually the outside reflected exactly what He said and *as He is, so are we in this world* (1 John 4:17).

Once you sow the seed, you must fight the feelings of discouragement when it appears to be no growth. It is very tempting to give up after a prolonged time of seeing no signs of change. You've done all you know to do…spiritually, you've prepared the ground, treated the soil with the best fertilizer, planted the seed, consistently watered and pulled up the weeds and even talked to the plant. After all that time, care and attention, there's no change and you are now tempted to call it quits. Yet there is a resolve that's needed to endure the dormant season. We must not allow the time of dormancy to put us in doubt, fear or anxiety about *if* it will happen. These will undoubtedly choke the seed and could potentially cause death to the seed that's being cultivated.

Some people give up too soon. It may take weeks. It may take months. It may even take years, but eventually, the roots

## Developed Through Dirt

will take hold and your "tree" will grow. And when it does, it will grow in remarkable ways. I know it's easier said than done but I would be remiss if I didn't say it again. HOLD ON, DON'T QUIT! Keep on fighting; keep on doing what's right. The wait will not be in vain.

We can look at the growth pattern of the Chinese Bamboo tree. There is no indication of growth for several years. Then in the fifth year, the tree experiences great increase. While most trees grow annually over a period of years, the Chinese Bamboo tree doesn't break through the ground for the first four years; all its activities are happing underground, beyond what the natural eye can see. It is developing a strong root system and foundation for the growth that will come. Then, in the fifth year, in a period of just five weeks, the tree grows upwards of 90 feet tall.

How many of us feel like our lives seem to parallel the Chinese Bamboo tree? For months and even years there's no tangible evidence that things are progressing, and then, all of the sudden, things take off for you. Breakthroughs come in your health. Increase comes to your finances. There is no more toil in your thoughts. You begin to see success and progress in your business. Healing and wholeness is manifested in your relationships. If it hasn't happened YET, keep holding onto the promises of God. It ***WILL*** happen!

## Rich Dirt, Bountiful Harvest

To receive this exponential increase, it requires steadfast faith. Just as those who plant Chinese Bamboo trees must have faith that eventually the tree will break through, so too must we have the same kind of faith in our dreams and destiny. It will come to pass no matter how long it takes. It's our human nature to want to see immediate harvest from what we plant; it does not happen like that *most* of the time. Not waiting and trying to circumvent the process will stunt the growth because the roots didn't go down deep enough to support the tree.

Waiting for harvest and manifestation is not always easy to do. Society has conditioned us to expect instant gratification. From microwaves to mobile salon services, we want what we want, when we want it. Don't get me wrong, I appreciate speed and efficiency but the best things and the greatest quality are resultant of a methodical, tedious process that takes time. Cubic zirconias have the same outward appearance as a diamond but it didn't go through the same process. Cubics are mass produced over a relatively short amount of time. Diamonds, on the other hand, go through a major pressurized, slow process, yet the final result is a high quality, high valued product which continues to increase in value over time.

To get the best quality, it is going to take time, so it's best to wait. Waiting is not a passive process. Contrary to popular belief, waiting is anything but idle. Waiting is an act of faith. Waiting is just as important, and in some instances, even more important than the end result that you are seeking. Waiting is a time of training, development, maturation and planning. It's more to waiting than sitting and counting down the time to your breakthrough. Waiting God's way is engaging and progressive. This is a season of deepening your faith and learning how to trust in God and His faithfulness.

During this time, consistently spend *quality* time in the presence of God. I emphasize quality because some people can spend the bulk of their prayer time complaining. This is counterproductive, as it gets you nowhere. Prayer, praise and worship will prove to be your necessary fortification, as many times waiting is laced with periods of darkness and disappointments. Pay it forward in praise. Praise in faith. There may be no evidence of an end to your waiting, but praise God as if you were already delivered. Praise through the pain. Worship instead of worrying. Yes, I've said it before but some people need a few reminders to praise their way through the pain. Another pivotal tool to aid in the wait is to feed on the Word so that during times of adversity, the Word will rise up and come out to counterattack the lies of the enemy.

During the wait, it is easy to get caught up with what you are going through and when you will get out of it. Don't be so anxious to get out of waiting that you miss the lessons, preparation, healing, growth and journey. Change your view; when you are faced with a situation, you only see from a limited eye level. It's narrow and you can't see much to the left or right, front or back. As you continue to keep your focus on God, He will help elevate you above the circumstances. You will then begin to see the bigger picture and it's nothing like you had initially imagined; it looks totally different than when you were facing it head on.

Secondly, when you begin to go above the situation, it is not as big as it was initially projected to you. As you magnify (to make bigger) God, the smaller the situation appears. You will start to see how big God is compared to your problems!

Thirdly, don't take up residence where you are; you are just passing through this hard place! There is nothing worse than making a permanent home to a place where you were supposed to just go through on a temporary basis. What you see as a disappointment is actually a divine appointment that God is using to bring to deliverance to many people. You are the decoy to give God access into the situation! Yes....YOU! Never underestimate the power of one. God used Joshua to lead the nation of Israel, Elijah changed the weather pattern for years, Ruth saved her nation, Moses delivered Israel, and Joseph kept Egypt from famine while the rest of the world was suffering. Yes others helped to make it happen but God initiated the order with one person and each of them went through a waiting process.

We can look at our perfect example, Jesus Christ. His waiting season was quite lengthy. Jesus sowed seed for 33 years and did not see a huge harvest but after He went through the worst time of His life and rose from the dead, He began to see the manifestation and harvest from the seeds He had sown. Thousands of years later, He is still receiving the harvest of seeds sown.

God will give you dreams, assignments, visions and plans that are too big for you so that you have no option but to wait on Him to make it happen in His timing. You could very well accomplish things on your own but the fullness of your destiny cannot be reached independent of God's timing and His divine assistance.

Do you realize you're not the only one still waiting on the manifestation of a promise? Even with all that Jesus went through and with what has already manifested for Him, He is still waiting on the harvest of certain promises that are yet to be fulfilled.

### *Philippians 2:10*

*Every knee shall bow and every tongue shall confess that Jesus Christ is Lord.*

### *1 Thessalonians 4:16*

*For the Lord Himself shall descend from Heaven with a shout.*

# Rich Dirt, Bountiful Harvest

## *Revelations 21:1*

*I saw a new Heaven and a new earth.*

So if Jesus is still waiting, then who are you?! What makes you think you won't have to go through a process and time of waiting? Sorry, it had to be said. I understand there's a great call on your life, you are destined to do great things, and you possess great faith. That's wonderful, beautiful even! Yet in addition to this great faith, there is going to be a waiting, just as Jesus is still waiting. Looks like you're in good company!

Speaking of callings, do you not realize there is a price to pay to carry the anointing and operate in the fullness of the calling God has for you? So that waiting season is for the sake of the call of God on your life to work out your "me-focused" mentality and work into you a Kingdom-focused mentality. In Exodus 30, it speaks of a special blend of oil (which represents the anointing) named calamus oil that God required Moses to use when he was consecrating the Tabernacle and tools that were to be used (Exodus 30:23-33). The calamus oil is significant because of the process it undergoes and the place of origin. The plant that produces the oil is sown in a well-watered terrain. Once the plant has taken root, the farmer completely floods the field. After the water subsides, it is flooded again. These adverse conditions are the optimal environment for the plant's growth.

## Developed Through Dirt

When it is determined that the plant has fully developed, it is removed from the soil (its source of nutrients) and left out to dry (THE WAIT). After the calamus has fully dried out, it must go through a beating and pressing to release the fragrance and oil. The more it is beaten, the more fragrant it becomes; if the plant is left as it is and does not go through the process, it produces a putrid odor. The greater the applied pressure, the more oil and fragrance is released from the plant. Don't fight or reject what God is doing in your life by not allowing the challenges of life to greet you. He is working to produce a fragrance and oil in you that will bring honor to Him.

I can tell you without any doubt, the waiting and developing season will be for your good. Although I went through many injustices, hardships, tests and troubles, I found the key to maximizing the wait...conforming to God's plan and appreciating the process. Through perseverance and a sheer will to live out my purpose, God graciously manifested deliverance in so many areas of my life. I came to the realization that sometimes what God promises is a part of a larger plan; I just happen to be the vessel and conduit He has chosen to use to help make it happen. It's about me but it's not all about me. My natural mind may not have totally understood the who, what, when, where and why of this process BUT my spirit knew God's plan was causing me to overcome and be victorious in life.

## Rich Dirt, Bountiful Harvest

First and foremost, the depth of my love and appreciation for God as my Heavenly Father has taken me to a place spiritually that I wouldn't have known had I not become intimate with the pressures from the process. I can truly say I *know* Him. There is an intimacy that is only gained through the fire. Through this development, I have learned how to forgive past feelings and love beyond emotions. Personal suffering tends to heighten our awareness of other people's pain and help us minister and care for them. My antenna is sensitized to the suffering of people and compels me to pray and encourage them.

God has restored me to a place well beyond where I was when the battles ensued. He's allowed me to journey along a career path that was not on my radar at all but it has opened up so many doors of opportunities professionally but that was merely a covert operation! I know the bigger plan is for me to manifest the Kingdom everywhere I go. I was allowed to hold a monthly Bible Study at work. As resistant as I was when God first instructed me to hold the Bible Study, I thoroughly enjoyed the time of teaching and studying with my co-workers. To unashamedly share our faith with one another while at work is a liberating feeling that is difficult to put into words. Through the Bible Study, people have accepted Jesus as their Lord and Savior. We have seen healings and answers to prayers manifest. The attendees became bolder in their witness with other co-workers.

## Developed Through Dirt

I now look at my job as a mission field and ask God to direct me to those who need an encounter with His love. BE CAREFUL FOR WHAT YOU ASK!!! He continues to answer this prayer by way of difficult people! I quickly remind myself, it's not about me; I'm merely a dispenser of His love and people are to partake of the fruit I've been graced to have *developed through dirt*.

# Endnotes

Chapter 2

1. "Shock and Awe; Achieving Rapid Dominance." Harlan Ullman, James Wade, Jr. October 1996.
2. Shock and Awe Military Tactic.
   https://en.wikipedia.org/wiki/Shock_and_awe
3. Blue Letter Bible.
   https://www.blueletterbible.org/lang/lexicon/lexicon.cfm?Strongs=G5392&t=KJV

Chapter 5

1. "On the Physical Death of Jesus Christ." William D. Edwards, MD; Wesley J. Gabel, MD; Floyd E. Hosmer. Journal of the American Medical Association. March 21, 1986—Volume 255, No. 11.

Chapter 6

1. "The Battle: A New History of Waterloo." *Alessandro Barbero*. 2005. Walker & Company.
2. "Arthur Wellesley, 1st Duke of Wellington."
   https://en.wikipedia.org/wiki/Arthur_Wellesley,_1st_Duke_of_Wellington#cite_note-Wellesley.2C_p._16-1

Chapter 7

1. Bible Study Notes. http://www.biblestudytools.com/lexicons/greek/kjv/soteria.html
2. "Walking in War." http://clgonline.org/walking-war-ephesians-610-20/

# Prayer of Salvation

You may be facing life's adversities without the assurance that your troubles have an expiration date. Without a personal relationship with the Lord Jesus Christ, He is not obligated to help you out of your troubles. The only prayer He is obligated to answer from a nonbeliever is Lord save me (Romans 10:13).

You may think your past is too much to forgive. Trust me, your past is no match for the power of Jesus' redemptive blood. There were some in the Bible whose pasts were not pretty. Lying, cussing, ear-cutting, Christ-denying, faithless Peter was one of the misfit disciples who had a very checkered past yet God's grace and love compelled him to become the first preacher of the Church. Moses, the adopted child who murdered and tried to give every excuse to run from the calling on his life and even rejected God's leading five times eventually got it together and became the spearhead of leading the children of Israel out of slavery. Rahab, the town's harlot, was used by God to save Joshua and Caleb. David, the philandering adulterous murderer, is revered as one of the greatest worshippers and warriors in any lifetime. Ruth went through a season of mourning, grief and depression from the loss of her husband yet she found love again, remarried, and she and Boaz produced the lineage of the great King David and King Jesus! Paul, a terrorist, heinous killer of Christians and avid Jesus hater became converted and was one of the greatest examples of how one encounter with Jesus Christ can change your life forever. If God can use all of these flawed individuals, your situation is not impossible. He can clean you and make you fit for the Master's use in the Kingdom.

If you are ready to join the family of God, simply pray this prayer out loud:

*Lord Jesus, I believe You are the Son of God who died for my sins. I confess with my mouth and believe in my heart that God raised You from the dead. Forgive me of all my sins. Be Lord of my life for the rest of my life.*
*Amen.*

If you prayed that prayer with a sincere heart, you are now saved. Hallelujah! Now it's important for you to find a church home that can help you grow and succeed in your spiritual walk. If you do not know of one, send an email to info@scribrpublicationsinc.com and they will connect you with a church in your area.

# Biography

Charity A. Morris, a native of Chicago, IL, is the fourth of six children born to Apostles David and Dorothy Nelson of New Destiny of Faith Ministry in Louisville, KY.

Charity received Christ into her heart in August 1985, at the age of 7. As a child and even today, one of her greatest and strongest spiritual mentors has been her mother, Dorothy, who has been effectively ministering The Word of God and spreading the God's love for over 30 years.

Charity is a dynamic teacher of God's Word who has a gifted ability to teach with clarity, simplicity, revelation and power. She has been blessed to travel throughout the U.S., Europe and Africa assisting with mission programs and ministering The Word of God.

She holds a B.A. in Psychology and an A.A. in French from Indiana University Northwest. In 2009, she also graduated from the Joseph Business School, under the leadership of Dr. Bill Winston, Pastor of Living Word Christian Center. Charity's entrepreneurial gifts manifested as she started her own publishing company, Scribe Publications, and also TDT Consulting Firm, a business strategy company.

Charity's work is her worship. Her heartbeat is seeing people experience the fullness of God. She is passionate about expanding God's Kingdom. Charity is the wife of Elder Gary Morris of Marvelous Light Christian Ministries. Together they have four beautiful children and reside in Georgia. If you would like to book Charity to speak at your conference, service, or event, please email info@charitymorris.org and we will get back to you within 24 hours.

www.ingramcontent.com/pod-product-compliance
Lightning Source LLC
Chambersburg PA
CBHW070625300426
44113CB00010B/1665